Essential

CHINESE

Speak Chinese With Confidence

Philip Yungkin Lee

Revised by
Shun-Yao Chang

TUTTLE Publishing
Tokyo | Rutland, Vermont | Singapore

The Tuttle Story: "Books to Span the East and West"

Most people are surprised to learn that the world's largest publisher of books on Asia had its humble beginnings in the tiny American state of Vermont. The company's founder, Charles E. Tuttle, belonged to a New England family steeped in publishing. And his first love was naturally books—especially old and rare editions.

Immediately after WW II, serving in Tokyo under General Douglas MacArthur, Tuttle was tasked with reviving the Japanese publishing industry. He later founded the Charles E. Tuttle Publishing Company, which thrives today as one of the world's leading independent publishers.

Though a westerner, Tuttle was hugely instrumental in bringing a knowledge of Japan and Asia to a world hungry for information about the East. By the time of his death in 1993, Tuttle had published over 6,000 books on Asian culture, history and art—a legacy honored by the Japanese emperor with the "Order of the Sacred Treasure," the highest tribute Japan can bestow upon a non-Japanese.

With a backlist of 1,500 titles, Tuttle Publishing is more active today than at any time in its past—inspired by Charles Tuttle's core mission to publish fine books to span the East and West and provide a greater understanding of each.

Published by Tuttle Publishing, an imprint of Periplus Editions (HK) Ltd.

www.tuttlepublishing.com

Copyright © 2013 Periplus Editions

ISBN 978-0-8048-4242-6

First edition
19 18 17 16 15 14 13
10 9 8 7 6 5 4 3 2 1
1304MP

Printed in Singapore

TUTTLE PUBLISHING® is a registered trademark of Tuttle Publishing, a division of Periplus Editions (HK) Ltd.

Distributed by

North America, Latin America & Europe
Tuttle Publishing
364 Innovation Drive
North Clarendon, VT 05759-9436 U.S.A.
Tel: 1 (802) 773-8930
Fax: 1 (802) 773-6993
info@tuttlepublishing.com
www.tuttlepublishing.com

Japan
Tuttle Publishing
Yaekari Building, 3rd Floor, 5-4-12 Osaki
Shinagawa-ku, Tokyo 141 0032
Tel: (81) 3 5437-0171
Fax: (81) 3 5437-0755
sales@tuttle.co.jp
www.tuttle.co.jp

Asia Pacific
Berkeley Books Pte. Ltd.
61 Tai Seng Avenue #02-12,
Singapore 534167
Tel: (65) 6280-1330
Fax: (65) 6280-6290
inquiries@periplus.com.sg
www.periplus.com

Contents

Introduction   5

Pronunciation guide   6

Basic grammar   8

1. The Basics   **15**

1.1 Personal details   16
1.2 Today or tomorrow?   17
1.3 What time is it?   20
1.4 One, two, three...   22
1.5 The weather   24
1.6 Here, there...   26
1.7 What does that sign say?   28
1.8 Legal holidays   29
1.9 Telephone alphabets   31

2. Meet and Greet   **33**

2.1 Greetings   34
2.2 Asking a question   36
2.3 How to reply   38
2.4 Thank you   40
2.5 I'm sorry   41
2.6 What do you think?   41

3. Small Talk   **44**

3.1 Introductions   45
3.2 I beg your pardon?   49
3.3 Starting/ending a conversation   50
3.4 A chat about the weather   51

3.5 Hobbies   51
3.6 Invitations   52
3.7 Paying a compliment   54
3.8 Intimate comments/ questions   55
3.9 Congratulations and condolences   56
3.10 Arrangements   57
3.11 Being the host(ess)   57
3.12 Saying good-bye   58

4. Eating Out   **59**

4.1 At the restaurant   60
4.2 Ordering   62
4.3 The bill   66
4.4 Complaints   67
4.5 Paying a compliment   68
4.6 Requests   68
4.7 Drinks   69
4.8 The menu   70

5. Getting Around   **71**

5.1 Asking directions   72
5.1 Traffic signs   74
5.3 The car   75
    The parts of a car   *76-77*
5.4 The gas station   75
5.5 Breakdowns and repairs   78
5.6 Bicycles/mopeds   80
    The parts of a bicycle   *82-83*

5.7	Renting a vehicle	81
5.8	Getting a lift	84

6. Arrival and Departure **86**

6.1	General	87
6.2	Customs	88
6.3	Luggage	90
6.4	Tickets	91
6.5	Information	92
6.6	Airports	94
6.7	Subway trains	96
6.8	Long-distance trains	98
6.9	Buses	100
6.10	Taxis	101

7. A Place to Stay **105**

7.1	General	106
7.2	Hotels/hostels/budget accommodations	107
7.3	Requests	111
7.4	Complaints	113
7.5	Departure	115

8. Money Matters **117**

8.1	Banks	118
8.2	Settling the bill	120

9. Mail, Phone and Internet **121**

9.1	Mail	122
9.2	Telephone	124
9.3	Internet/email	126

10. Shopping **128**

10.1	Shopping conversations	130
10.2	Food	132

10.3	Clothing and shoes	133
10.4	At the hairdresser	135

11. Tourist Activities **138**

11.1	Sightseeing	139
11.2	Places of interest	141
11.3	Going out	144
11.4	Nightlife	146
11.5	Cultural performance	146
11.6	Booking tickets	148

12. Sports Activities **150**

12.1	Sporting questions	151
12.2	By the waterfront	151
12.3	In the snow	153

13. Health Matters **155**

13.1	Calling a doctor	156
13.2	What's wrong?	157
13.3	The consultation	158
13.4	Medications and prescriptions	163
13.5	At the dentist	164

14. Emergencies **166**

14.1	Asking for help	167
14.2	Lost items	168
14.3	Accidents	169
14.4	Theft	170
14.5	Missing person	170
14.6	The police	172

15. English-Chinese Word List **176-208**

Introduction

● **Welcome to the Tuttle Essential Language series, covering all of the most popular world languages. These books are basic guides in communicating in the language. They're concise, accessible and easy to understand, and you'll find them indispensable on your trip abroad to get you where you want to go, pay the right prices and do everything you've been planning to do.**

Each guide is divided into 15 themed sections and starts with a pronunciation table which explains the phonetic pronunciation to all the words and sentences you'll need to know, and a basic grammar guide which will help you construct basic sentences in your chosen language. At the end of this book is an extensive English–Chinese word list.

Throughout the book you'll come across boxes with a 👋 beside them. These are designed to help you if you can't understand what your listener is saying to you. Hand the book over to them and encourage them to point to the appropriate answer to the question you are asking.

Other boxes in the book—this time without the symbol—give listings of themed words with their English translations.

For extra clarity, we have put all phonetic pronunciations of the foreign language terms in bold.

This book covers all subjects you are likely to come across during the course of a visit, from reserving a room for the night to ordering food and drink at a restaurant and what to do if your car breaks down or you lose your money. With over 2,000 commonly used words and essential sentences at your fingertips you can rest assured that you will be able to get by in all situations, so let *Essential Chinese* become your passport to learning to speak with confidence!

Pronunciation guide

The imitated pronunciation should be read as if it were English, bearing in mind the following main points:

Consonants

b, d, f, g, h, k, l, m, n, p, s, t, w, y as in English

c   like English **ts** in **its**

j   like English **j** in **j**eep

q   like English **ch** in **ch**eer, with a strong puff of air

r   like English **ur** in leis**ur**e, with the tongue rolled back

x   like English **see** (whole word)

z   like English **ds** in ki**ds**

ch like English **ch** in **ch**urch, with the tongue rolled back and a strong puff of air

sh like English **sh** in **sh**e, with the tongue rolled back

zh like English **j**, with the tongue rolled back

Vowels

a   like English **a** in f**a**r

e   like English **u** in f**ur**

i   like English **ee** in f**ee**

o   like English **o** in f**o**r

u   like English **ue** in s**ue**

ü   like French **u**

Tones

A tone is a variation in pitch by which a syllable can be pronounced. In Chinese, a variation of pitch or tone changes the meaning of the word. There are four tones each marked by a diacritic. In addition there is a neutral tone which does not carry any tone marks. Below is a tone chart which describes tones using the 5-degree notation. It divides the range of pitches from lowest (1) to highest (5). Note that the neutral tone is not shown on the chart as it is affected by the tone that precedes it.

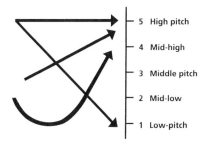

The first tone is a high-level tone represented by a level tone mark ▬.

The second tone is a high-rising tone represented by a rising tone mark ✓.

The third tone is a low-dipping tone represented by a dish-like tone mark ∨.

The fourth tone is a high-falling tone represented by a falling tone mark ╲.

The neutral tone is pronounced light and soft in comparison to other tones and is not marked by any tone mark. A syllable is said to take on a neutral tone when it forms part of a word or is placed in various parts of a sentence.

Basic grammar

Compared to many European languages, Chinese grammar is quite simple. There are no verb conjugations, no plurals, no gender in nouns, no articles and the sentence order is intuitive to English speakers. This section presents Chinese grammar in parts of speech familiar to English speakers.

1 Word order

More often than not, Chinese word order is the same as in English:

subject – verb – object

| **Wǒ** | **xué** | **Hànyǔ** | 我-学-汉语 | I | study | Chinese |

2 Nouns and pronouns

Mandarin words are mostly made up of two characters and nouns are no different. No distinction is made between singular and plural nouns. When it is necessary to distinguish plurals, this is done through the use of measure words which indicate the number of items involved.

For example, the word for "hotel," **bīn'guǎn** 宾馆 can be either singular or plural unless it is necessary to indicate that there are more than one. Thus,

yì jiā bīn'guǎn	一家宾馆	"one hotel"
liǎng jiā bīn'guǎn	两家宾馆	"two hotels"
sān jiā bīn'guǎn	三家宾馆	"three hotels"

In the above examples, the noun **bīn'guǎn** 宾馆 "hotel" is qualified by a number with the appropriate measure word **jiā** 家, which indicates whether or not it is singular or plural. You will notice that whereas the number **èr** 二 "two" is used in counting, e.g., **yī, èr, sān**... 一二三 "one, two, three ..." the word **liǎng** 两 "a couple of" replaces **èr** 二 "two" where a measure word is used.

Like nouns, Chinese pronouns do not change form whether they are used as subjects or objects. Simple personal pronouns are: **wǒ** 我 "I/me," **nǐ** 你 "you," **tā** 他 "he/him," **tā** 她 "she/her" and **tā** 它 "it" (the last three pronouns share the same pronunciation but are written with different characters).

Unlike nouns, however, Chinese pronouns can take on plural forms with the addition of the suffix **-men** 们, making the above examples into **wǒmen** 我们 "we/us," **nǐmen** 你们 "you" (plural), **tāmen** 他们 "they/them" (either all male or mixed) and **tāmen** 她们 "they/them" (all female). Similarly, the pronoun for animals or insects is **tāmen** 它们 "they/them." The suffix **-men** 们 is added to nouns only sparingly in greetings, e.g., **nǚshìmen**, **xiānshengmen** 女士们、先生们 "ladies and gentlemen," as it is unnecessary to indicate plural forms in nouns.

In addition to personal pronouns, there are demonstrative pronouns. For example, **zhè** 这 "this" and **nà** 那 "that." It is important to note that a plural measure word **xiē** 些 is added to give the plural forms of these pronouns: **zhèxiē** 这些 "these" and **nàxiē** 那些 "those," so it is not a plural form in the sense that **-men** 们 is used.

3 Possessives and measure words

To make a possessive out of a noun or pronoun, simply add the particle **de** 的. Thus,

dǎoyóu de	导游的	"the tour guide's"
Lǐ xiǎojie de	李小姐的	"Miss Li's"
wǒde	我的	"my" or "mine"
nǐde	你的	"your" (singular) or "yours"
tāde	他/她的	"his/her"
wǒmende	我们的	"our"
nǐmende	你们的	"your" (plural) or "yours" (plural)
tāmende	他们的	"their" or "theirs"

You have learned to use measure words in conjunction with numbers to indicate the plural form of a noun. In English we say "a slice/loaf of bread," "a piece/ream of paper," "a school of fish" etc. In Chinese this usage applies to all nouns in order to specify number, e.g., "a book" is **yìběn shū** 一本书, "a table" is **yì zhāng zhuōzi** 一张桌子 and "two chairs" is **liǎng bǎ yǐzi** 两把椅子. As you can see from the above examples, there isn't one unique measure word for each noun; measure words tend to describe classes of objects with similar characteristics. Thus the word **běn** 本 describes bound books, **zhāng** 张 describes wide, flat objects of many types such as tables, paper, bedsheets, etc., and **bǎ** describes things with handles including chairs, knives, forks, etc. Luckily for beginners of the language, there is a general-use measure word **ge** 个 which is used in simple phrases like **zhè ge** 这个 "this one," **nà ge** 那个 "that one," **nǎ ge** 哪个 "which one" or **jǐ ge** 几个 "how many (items)?"

4 Verbs

Chinese verbs are not conjugated, but keep one simple form regardless of the subject or tense. Thus the verb **chī** 吃 "eat" is the same whether the subject is I, you, he/she or they, and whether the action took place yesterday or will happen two days from now. There are ways to indicate tense in Chinese sentences, e.g., the use of time words before the verb, the use of the particles **guo** 过 and **le** 了 to indicate past and completed action, and the use of **yào** 要 and **huì** 会 to indicate future action. For example,

• The use of time words before the verb:

Wǒ zuótiān chī jiǎozi.	我昨天吃饺子	"Yesterday I ate dumplings"
Wǒ jīntiān chī jiǎozi.	我今天吃饺子	"Today I eat dumplings"
Wǒ míngtiān chī jiǎozi.	我明天吃饺子	"Tomorrow I'll be eating dumplings"

Note that the Chinese verb **chī** 吃 "eat" does not change to indicate tense; this is done through the use of **zuótiān** 昨天 "yesterday," **jīntiān** 今天 "today" and **míngtiān** 明天 "tomorrow."

- The use of the particle **guo** 过 after the verb to indicate action occurred in unspecified time in the past:

Wǒ chīguo jiǎozi.   我吃过饺子   "I've eaten dumplings previously"

- The use of the particle **le** 了 after the verb to indicate action has just been recently completed:

Wǒ chīle jiǎozi. 我吃了饺子 "I've just eaten (the) dumplings"

- The use of the aspect partices **yào** 要 "want" or **huì** 会 "will/shall" before the verb to indicate future action:

Wǒ yào chī jiǎozi.   我要吃饺子   "I'm going to eat (the) dumplings"

Wǒ huì chī (nàxiē) jiǎozi.   我会吃(那些)饺子的。   "I'll be eating (the) dumplings"

5 Adjectives

Adjectives in Chinese are simple as they don't need to agree in gender or number with the nouns they modify. They are sometimes called stative verbs as they incorporate the verb "to be" in the sentence. In their positive form, adjectives are generally preceded by the adverb **hěn** 很 "very." Thus **Wǒ hěn gāoxìng** 我很高兴 means "I'm very happy."

   When adjectives modify nouns in phrases they generally precede the noun, often using the particle **de** 的 in between. For example,

xiǎo xióngmāo	小熊猫	"a small panda"
zāng yīfu	脏衣服	"soiled clothings"
hǎo péngyou	好朋友	"good friends"
měilì de fēngjǐng	美丽的风景	"beautiful scenery"
míngguì de lǐwù	名贵的礼物	"expensive gift"
tǎoyàn de wénzi	讨厌的蚊子	"annoying mosquitoes"

6 Adverbs

Just as adjectives precede the nouns they modify, adverbs are placed before verbs, adjectives or other adverbs to express time, degree, scope, repetition, possibility, negotiation and tone of speech. Common examples are: **hěn** 很 "very," **yě** 也 "also," **bǐjiào** 比较 "rather," **jiù** 就 "then," **zǒng** 总 "always." For example,

Chángchéng hěn cháng.	长城很长	"The Great Wall is long."
Wǒ yě xiǎng chángchang Běijīng kǎoyā.	我也想尝尝北京烤鸭。	"I'd also like to try Beijing Duck."
Shànghǎi xiàtiān bǐjiào rè.	上海夏天比较热。	"Shanghai is rather hot in summer."
Nǐ xiān zǒu, wǒ mǎshàng jiù lái.	你先走，我马上就来。	"You go first, I'll catch up with you later."
Wǔyuè de shíhou, zhèlǐ zǒng xiàyǔ.	五月的时候，这里总下雨。	"Around May, it is always raining here."

7 Negatives

There are generally two particles that are used for forming the negative in Chinese. They are **bù/bú** 不 and **méi** 没. The one you're most likely to need is **bù** 不, sometimes pronounced as **bú** 不 when it precedes a word in the fourth tone. Both **bù** 不 and **bú** 不 are placed before verbs or adjectives to indicate negation in simple present tense. To indicate negation in the past tense, i.e., an action that has not been completed, **méi** 没 is used.

Guǎngzhōu dōngtiān bù lěng.	广州冬天不冷。	"Guangzhou is not cold in winter."
Shànghǎi dōngtiān bú xiàxuě.	上海冬天不下雪。	"It does not snow in Shanghai in winter."
Qùnián Běijīng méi xiàxuě.	去年北京没下雪。	"Last year it didn't snow in Beijing."

8 Interrogatives

There are three basic ways to ask questions in Chinese. The most common way is to add the particle **ma** 吗 to the end of a declarative sentence.

Nǐ lèi ma?	你累吗？	"Are you tired?"
Nǐ gāoxìng ma?	你高兴吗？	"Are you happy?"

The second way is to use the choice-type question which presents the listener with two opposite alternatives.

Nǐ lèi bu lèi?	你累不累？	"Are you tired?"
Nǐ gāo(xìng) bu gāoxìng?	你高(兴)不高兴？	"Are you happy?"

The third way is by using an interrogative pronoun. Examples are **shéi/shuí** 谁 "who," **shénme** 什么 "what," **zěnme** 怎么 "how," **nǎ** 哪 "which," **nǎli/nǎr** 那里/哪儿 "where," **wèishénme** 为什么 "why," **jǐ diǎnzhōng/shénme shíhou** 几点钟/什么时候 "when."

1.	**Nǐ shì shéi/shuí?**	你是谁？	"Who are you?"
2.	**Nǐ jiào shénme míngzi?**	你叫什么名字？	"What's your name?"
3.	**Nǐ zěnme jìnlái de?**	你怎么进来的？	"How did you get in?"
4.	**Nǐ cóng nǎ ge mén jìnlái de?**	你从哪个门进来的？	"Which door did you get in?"
5.	**Nǐ bàba māma zài nǎli?**	你爸爸妈妈在哪里？	"Where are your parents?"
6.	**Nǐ wèishénme bù shuōhuà?**	你为什么不说话？	"Why aren't you saying anything?"
7.	**Xiànzài jǐ diǎnzhōng le?**	现在几点钟了？	"What's the time now?"
8.	**Nǐ shénme shíhou jìnlái de?**	你什么时候进来的？	"When did you come in here?"

In answering a question involving the interrogative pronoun, follow the grammar of the question and note its word order, changing the subject of the sentence where appropriate, e.g., **nǐ** 你

"you" becomes **wǒ** 我 "I" when you answer a question. Then, just substitute the noun for the interrogative pronoun. For example, when you asked the lost child who wandered into your room the above questions, the answers to some of these questions may be:

1. **Wǒ shī Xiǎohuá.**   我是小华。   "I'm Xiaohua."

2. **Wǒ jiào Wáng Xiǎohuá.**   我叫王小华。   "My name is Wang Xiaohua."

3. **Wǒ mílùle.**   我迷路了。   "I'm lost."

4. **Wǒ cóng nà ge mén jìnlái de.**   我从那个门 进来的。   'I got in from that door."

5. **Wǒ bàba māma zài lǚguǎn.**   我爸爸妈妈在 旅馆。   "My parents are in the hotel."

6. **Wǒ mílùle, wǒ pà.**   我迷路了, 我怕。   "I'm lost, I'm scared."

7. **Wǒ bù zhīdao shì jǐ diǎnzhōng.**   我不知道是几 点钟。   "I don't know the time."

8. **Wǒ jìnlái hěn jiǔ le.**   我进来很久了。   "I've been here a long time."

9 Yes/no answers

For questions ending with the interrogative particle **ma** 吗, take away the particle **ma** 吗, and answer according to the situation that you find yourself in. There are no specific words in Chinese for "yes" and "no." The closest equivalent is **shìde** 是的 and **búshì** 不是 respectively. Usually, when the Chinese are asked a question, they repeat the verb used in the question to answer in the affirmative. If they want to answer in the negative, they add **bù** 不 before the verb used in the sentence. Similarly, for choice-type question the opposite alternatives can be either "yes" or "no." Thus,

"Yes" answer: **Hěn lèi.**   很累。   "Yes, I'm very tired."

"No" answer: **Bú lèi.**   不累。   "No, I'm not tired."

"Yes" answer: **Gāoxìng.**   高兴。   "Yes, I'm happy."

"No" answer: **Bù gāoxìng**   不高兴。   "No, I'm not happy."

1 The Basics

1.1	Personal details	16
1.2	Today or tomorrow?	17
1.3	What time is it?	20
1.4	One, two, three...	22
1.5	The weather	24
1.6	Here, there...	26
1.7	What does that sign say?	28
1.8	Legal holidays	29
1.9	Telephone alphabets	31

1. The Basics

1.1 Personal details

● **In China** the family name comes first and the given name next. Titles come after the name. For example, Mr Wang is **Wáng xiānsheng** 王先生 and Ms Wang is either **Wáng xiǎojie** 王小姐 or **Wáng nǚshì** 王女士. The title **tàitai** 太太 is given to married women and is placed after the husband's surname. This is the convention still used by Chinese women in Hong Kong, Macau, Taiwan and outside China. In Mainland China, however, Chinese women now do not adopt their husband's surname after marriage. Overseas Chinese and foreigners will have to get used to this new convention and address married women by their maiden name, e.g. if her surname is **Lǐ** 李 she should be addressed as **Lǐ xiǎojie** 李小姐 or **Lǐ dàjiě** 李大姐 (for older woman). However, you may even use the older title **tàitai** 太太 after the husband's surname in formal situations.

surname	**xìng** 姓
first name	**míngzi** 名字
initials	**xìngmíng suōxiě** 姓名缩写
address (street/number)	**dìzhǐ (jiē/ménpáihào)** 地址（街／门牌号）
postal code/town	**yóubié/chéngshì** 邮编／城市
sex (male/female)	**xìngbié (nán/nǚ)** 性别（男／女）
nationality/citizenship	**guójí** 国籍
date of birth	**chūshēng rìqī** 出生日期

place of birth	**chūshēng dìdiǎn** 出生地点
occupation	**zhíyè** 职业
marital status	**hūnyīn zhuàngkuàng** 婚姻状况
married/single	**yǐhūn/wèihūn** 已婚／未婚
widowed	**guǎfù/guānfū** 寡妇／鳏夫
(number of) children	**érnǚ (shùmù)** 儿女（数目）
passport/identity card/ driving license number	**hùzhào/shēnfènzhèng/jiàshǐzhízhào** **hàomǎ** 护照／身份证／驾驶执照号码
place and date of issue	**qiānfā dìdiǎn/qiānfā rìqī** 签发地点／签发日期
signature	**qiānmíng** 签名

1.2 Today or tomorrow?

What day is it today?	**Jīntiān shì xīngqījǐ?/lǐbàijǐ** 今天是星期几？／礼拜几？
Today's Monday	**Jīntiān shì xīngqīyī/lǐbàiyī** 今天是星期一／礼拜一
Tuesday	**xīngqī'èr/lǐbài'èr** 星期二／礼拜二
Wednesday	**xīngqīsān/lǐbàisān** 星期三／礼拜三
Thursday	**xīngqīsì/lǐbàisì** 星期四／礼拜四
Friday	**xīngqīwǔ/lǐbàiwǔ** 星期五／礼拜五

Saturday	**xīngqīliù/lǐbàiliù** 星期六／礼拜六
Sunday	**xīngqītiān/xīngqīrì, lǐbàitiān/lǐbàirì** 星期天／星期日、礼拜天／礼拜日
in January	**(zài) Yīyuè** （在）一月
since February	**Èryuèyǐlái** 二月以来
in spring	**(zài) chūntiān** （在）春天
in summer	**(zài) xiàtiān** （在）夏天
in autumn	**(zài) qiūtiān** （在）秋天
in winter	**(zài) dōngtiān** （在）冬天
2012	**Èrlíngyīèr nián** 二零一二年
the twentieth century	**Èrshí shìjì** 20 世纪
the twenty-first century	**Èrshíyī shìjì** 21 世纪
What's the date today?	**Jīntiān jǐhào?** 今天几号？
Today's the 24th	**Jīntiān shì èrshísì hào** 今天是24号
Wednesday 3 November	**Shíyīyuè sānhào, xīngqīsān** 十一月三号，星期三
in the morning	**(zài) zǎoshang** （在）早上
in the afternoon	**(zài) xiàwǔ** （在）下午
in the evening	**(zài) wǎnshang** （在）晚上

at night	**(zài) yèlǐ** （在）夜里
this morning	**jīntiān zǎoshang** 今天早上
this afternoon	**jīntiān xiàwǔ** 今天下午
this evening	**jīntiān wǎnshang** 今天晚上
tonight	**jīntiān wǎnshang** 今天晚上
last night	**zuótiān wǎnshang** 昨天晚上
tomorrow night	**míngtiān wǎnshang** 明天晚上
this week	**zhè ge xīngqī** 这个星期
last week	**shàng ge xīngqī** 上个星期
next week	**xià ge xīngqī** 下个星期
this month	**zhè ge yuè** 这个月
last month	**shàng ge yuè** 上个月
next month	**xià ge yuè** 下个月
this year	**jīnnián** 今年
last year	**qùnián** 去年
next year	**míngnián** 明年
in...days/weeks/ months/years	**tiān/xīngqī/yuè/nián...yǐhòu** 天／星期／月／年…以后

...weeks ago	**...(ge) xīngqī/lǐbài yǐqián** …（个）星期／礼拜以前
two weeks ago	**liǎng ge xīngqī yǐqián** 两个星期以前
two weeks ago	**liǎng ge lǐbài yǐqián** 两个礼拜以前
day off	**xiūjiàrì** 休假日

1.3 What time is it?

What time is it?	**Jǐdiǎn (zhōng) le?/Shénme shíhoule?** 几点(钟)了／什么时候了？
It's nine o'clock	**Jiǔ diǎn** 九点
five past ten	**shí diǎn wǔfēn/shí diǎn guò wǔfēn** 十点五分／十点过五分
a quarter past eleven	**shíyī diǎn yī kè/shíyī diǎn shíwǔ fēn** 十一点一刻／十一点十五分
twenty past twelve	**shí'èr diǎn èrshí fēn** 十二点二十分
half past one	**yí diǎn bàn/yī diǎn sānshí fēn** 一点半／一点三十分
twenty-five to three	**liǎng diǎn sānshíwǔ fēn/chà èrshíwǔ fēn sān diǎn** 两点三十五分／差二十五分三点
a quarter to four	**sān diǎn sìshíwǔ fēn/sān diǎn sān kè/chà yī kè sì diǎn** 三点四十五分／三点三刻／差一刻四点
ten to five	**sì diǎn wǔshí fēn/chà shífēn wǔ diǎn** 四点五十分／差十分五点
It's midday (twelve noon)	**zhōngwǔ le/shí'èr diǎn le** 中午了／十二点了

It's midnight	**wǎnshàng shí'èr diǎn** 晚上十二点
half an hour	**bàn ge zhōngtóu/bàn ge xiǎoshí** 半个钟头／半个小时
What time?	**Jǐ diǎn/Shénme shíhou?** 几点／什么时候？
What time can I come by?	**Wǒ jǐ diǎn kěyǐ guòlaí?** 我几点可以过来？
At...	**zài...** 在…
After...	**...yǐhòu** …以后
Before...	**...yǐqián** …以前
Between 4:00 and 5:00	**sì diǎn hé wǔ diǎn zhījiān** 四点和五点之间
From...to...	**cóng...dào...** 从…到…
In...minutes	**...fénzhōng yǐhòu** …分钟以后
an hour	**yí ge zhōngtóu/yí ge xiǎoshí yǐhòu** 一个钟头／一个小时以后
two hours	**liǎng ge zhōngtóu/liǎng ge xiǎoshí yǐhòu** 两个钟头／两个小时以后
a quarter of an hour	**yí kèzhōng/shíwǔ fēnzhōng yǐhòu** 一刻钟／十五分钟以后
three quarters of an hour	**sān kèzhōng/sìshí fēnzhōng yǐhòu** 三刻钟／四十五分钟以后
too early/late	**tài zǎo le/tài wǎn le** 太早了／太晚了
on time	**zhǔnshí/ànshí** 准时／按时

| summertime (daylight saving) | **xiàlìngshí** 夏令时 |
| wintertime | **dōngjì shíjiān** 冬季时间 |

1.4 One, two, three...

0	**líng** 零
1	**yī** 一
2	**èr** 二
3	**sān** 三
4	**sì** 四
5	**wǔ** 五
6	**liù** 六
7	**qī** 七
8	**bā** 八
9	**jiǔ** 九
10	**shí** 十
11	**shíyī** 十一
12	**shí'èr** 十二
13	**shísān** 十三
14	**shísì** 十四
15	**shíwǔ** 十五
16	**shíliù** 十六
17	**shíqī** 十七
18	**shíbā** 十八
19	**shíjiǔ** 十九
20	**èrshí** 二十
21	**èrshíyī** 二十一
22	**èrshí'èr** 二十二

30	sānshí	三十
31	sānshíyī	三十一
40	sìshí	四十
50	wǔshí	五十
60	liùshí	六十
70	qīshí	七十
80	bāshí	八十
90	jiǔshí	九十
100	yībǎi	一百
101	yībǎi líng yī	一百零一
110	yībǎi yīshí	一百一十
111	yībǎi yīshíyī	一百一十一
200	èrbǎi/ liǎngbǎi	二百／两百
300	sānbǎi	三百
400	sìbǎi	四百
500	wǔbǎi	五百
600	liùbǎi	六百
700	qībǎi	七百
800	bābǎi	八百
900	jiǔbǎi	九百
1,000	yīqiān	一千
1,100	yīqiān yībǎi	一千一百
2,000	èrqiān/liǎngqiān	二千／两千
10,000	yīqàn	一万
100,000	shíwàn	十万
1,000,000	(yī)bǎiwàn	（一）百万
10,000,000	(yī)qiānwàn	（一）千万
1st	dìyī	第一
2nd	dì'èr	第二

3rd	**dìsān** 第三
4th	**dìsì** 第四
once	**yí cì** 一次
twice	**liǎng cì** 两次
double	**liǎng bèi** 两倍
triple	**sān bèi** 三倍
half	**yíbān** 一半
a quarter	**sìfēnzhīyī** 四分之一
a third	**sānfēnzhīyī** 三分之一
some/a few	**yìxiē/jǐge** 一些／几个
2 + 4 = 6	**èr jiā sì děngyú liù** 二加四等于六
4 – 2 = 2	**sì jiā èr děngyú èr** 四减二等于二
2 x 4 = 8	**èr chéng sì děngyú bā** 二乘四等于八
4 ÷ 2 = 2	**sì chúyú èr děngyú èr** 四除于二等于二
even/odd	**shuāngshù/dānshù** 双数／单数
total	**yígòng** 一共

1.5 The weather

Is the weather going to be good/bad?	**Tiānqì huì hǎo ma?/huì huài ma?** 天气会好吗?／会坏吗?
Is it going to get colder/hotter?	**Tiānqì yào biàn lěng/rè le ba?** 天气要变冷／热了吧?
What temperature is it going to be?	**(Jīntiān) qìwēn duōshao dù?** （今天）气温多少度?
Is it going to rain?	**(Jīntiān) huì xiàyǔ ma?** （今天）会下雨吗?
Is there going to be a storm?	**(Jīntiān) huì yǒu fēngbào ma?** （今天）会有风暴吗?
Is it going to snow?	**(Jīntiān) huì xiàxuě ma?** （今天）会下雪吗?

Is it going to freeze?	**(Jīntiān) huì jiébīng ma?** （今天）会结冰吗？
Is the thaw setting in?	**Jiědòng le ma?** 解冻了吗？
Is it going to be foggy?	**(Jīntiān) huì xiàwù ma?** （今天）会下雾吗？
Is there going to be a thunderstorm?	**(Jīntiān) huì yǒu léiyǔ ma?** （今天）会有雷雨吗？
The weather's changing	**Tiānqì yào biànle** 天气要变了
It's going to be cold	**Tiān yào biàn lěng le** 天要变冷了
What's the weather going to be like today/tomorrow?	**Jīntiān/Míngtiān de tiānqì zěnmeyàng?** 今天／明天的天气怎么样？

下雨
xiàyǔ
rain

大雨
dàyǔ
heavy rain

晴朗
qínglǎng
sunny

很热
hěn rè
very hot

晴天
qíngtiān
fine

冰／结冰的
bīng/jiébīngde
ice/icy

霜／寒冷
**shuāng/
hánlěng**
frost/frosty

暴雨／倾盆大雨
bàoyǔ/qīngpén dàyǔ
downpour

又冷又潮湿
yòu lěng yòu cháoshī
cold and damp

蓝天／多云／阴天
lántiān/duōyún/yīntiān
clear skies/cloudy/overcast

（华氏）度
(huáshì) dù
...degrees (Fahrenheit)

（摄氏）度
(shèshì) dù
...degrees (Celsius)

零下…度
língxià...dù
...degrees (below zero)

和风／大风／狂风
héfēng/dàfēng/kuángfēng
moderate/strong/very strong winds

有霜
yǒu shuāng
frost

风
fēng
wind

暴风雨
bàofēngyǔ
storm

潮湿
cháoshī
humid

凉快
liángkuai
cool

下雪
xiàxuě
snow

阴冷的
yīnlěngde
bleak

闷热
mēn rè
sweltering/muggy

晴朗
qínglǎng
fine/clear

热风
rèfēng
heatwave

刮风的
guāfēngde
windy

飓风
jùfēng
hurricane

多云状态
duōyún zhuàngtài
cloudiness

雹子／冰雹 **báozi/bīngbáo** hail	夜间有霜 **yèjiān yǒu shuāng** overnight frost	闷人的 **mènrénde** stifling	晴／天晴 **qíng/** **tiānqíng** sunny day
大风 **dàfēng** gusts of wind	大雾／多雾的 **dàwù/duōwùde** fog/foggy	暖和的 **nuǎnhuode** mild	

1.6 Here, there...

See also 5.1 Asking directions

here, over here/there, over there	**zhèr/zhèlǐ, nàr/nàli** 这儿／这里，那儿／那里
somewhere	**mǒuchù** 某处
everywhere	**dàochù** 到处
far away/nearby	**yáoyuǎn/fùjìn** 遥远／附近
(on the) right/ (on the) left	**zài yòubiān/zài zuǒbiān** 在右边／在左边
to the right/left of	**kào yòubiān/kào zuǒbiān** 靠右边／靠左边
straight ahead	**yìzhí wǎng qián zǒu** 一直往前走
via	**jìngguò/yóu** 经过／由
in/to	**(zài)...lǐ/dào** （在）…里／到
on	**(zài)...shàng** （在）…上
under	**(zài)...xià** （在）…下
against	**gēn...xiāngduì** 跟…相对

opposite/facing	**duìmiàn** 对面
next to	**āizhe/(zài)...pángbiān** 挨着／（在）…旁边
near	**kàojìn** 靠近
in front of	**(zài)...qiánmiàn** （在）…前面
in the center	**(zài)...zhōngjiān** （在）…中间
forward	**xiàng qián** 向前
down	**xiàng xià** 向下
up	**xiàng shàng** 向上
inside	**lǐbiān** 里边
outside	**wàibiān** 外边
at the front	**(zài)...qiánmiàn** （在）…前面
at the back	**(zài)...hòumiàn** （在）…后面
in the north	**(zài)...běibiān** （在）…北边
to the south	**zài...yǐ nán** 在…以南
from the west	**(cóng)...xībiān** （从）…西边
from the east	**(cóng)...dōngbiān** （从）…东边

See 5.2 Traffic signs

The Basics

1

交通标志
jiāotōng biāozhì
traffic signs

出租
chūzū
for hire/rent

出售
chūshòu
for sale

卖完
màiwán
sold out

热水 / 冷水
rèshuǐ/lěngshuǐ
hot/cold water

非饮用水
fēiyǐnyòngshuǐ
water (not for
  drinking)

停用
tíngyòng
not in use

推
tuī
push

打开
dǎkāi
open

拉
lā
pull

洗手间
xǐshǒujiān
bathrooms

满 / 客满
mǎn/kèmǎn
full

邮局
yóujú
post office

高压电
gāo yā diàn
high voltage

问讯处
wènxùn chù
information

售票处
shòupiào chù
ticket office

收款处
shōukuǎn chù
cashier

免费入场
miǎnfèi rùchǎng
entrance (free)

当心恶狗
dāngxīn è gǒu
beware of the dog

油漆未干
yóuqī wèi gān
wet paint

危险
wéixiǎn
danger

无人
wúrén
vacant

入口
rùkǒu
entrance

紧急出口
jǐnjí chūkǒu
(emergency) exit

此路不通 / 禁止入内
cǐlù bùtōng/jìnzhǐ rùnèi
no access/no entry

警察(局) / 公安(局)
jǐngchá (jú)/gōng'ān (jú)
police

交通警察
jiāotōng jǐngchá
traffic police

候客 / 候机 / 候车
hóu kè/hóu jī/hóu chē
waiting room

医院
yīyuàn
hospital

急救室 / 事故急诊室
jíjiùshì/shìgù jízhěnshì
first aid/accident and
  emergency (hospital)

灭火局 / 消防局
mièhuǒjú/xiāofángjú
fire department

紧急刹车
jǐnjíshāchē
emergency brake

停止营业 / 休假 /
  装修施工
tíngzhǐ yíngyè/xiūjià/
  zhuāngxiū shīgōng
closed (for holiday/
  refurbishment)

禁止打猎 / 禁止钓鱼
jìnzhǐ dǎliè/jìnzhǐ diàoyú
no hunting/fishing

安全出口 / 自动楼梯
ānquán chūkǒu/zìdòng lóutī
fire escape/escalator

预订席 / 包席 **yùdìngxí/bāoxí** reserved	有人 **yǒurén** engaged	旅行咨询处 **lǚxíng zīxúnchù** tourist information bureau
宾馆 / 旅馆 **bīn'guǎn/lǚguǎn** hotel	行人 **xíngrén** pedestrians	请勿抽烟 / 请勿乱丢废屑 **qǐngwù chōuyān/qǐngwù luàndiū fèixiè** no smoking/no littering
待维修 **dài wéixiū** out of order	时刻表 **shíkèbiǎo** timetable	危险 / 易燃 / 致命 **wéixiǎn/yìrán/zhìmìng** danger/fire hazard/ danger to life
停（止） **tíng (zhǐ)** stop	兑换 **duìhuàn** exchange	请勿打扰 / 请勿触摸 **qǐngwù dǎrǎo/qǐngwù chùmō** please do not disturb/touch

1.8 Legal holidays

● **Apart from Chinese New Year** which is celebrated through-out China with two weeks off from work, other holidays are mostly observed in the cities with time off to celebrate the fes-tivities. There are two types of festivals, traditional and modern.

The former follow the lunar calendar which identifies the months sequentially as the First Month, the Second Month, etc. Chinese New Year or the Spring Festival varies every year but falls between the last 10 days of January and the first 10 days of February each year.

Modern holidays are historically linked to the New China with National Day (October 1) and Labor Day (May 1) heading the list. National Day and Labor Day are each celebrated with a week off work when people are encouraged to spend and go for holi-days in an attempt to stimulate the economy. On these occasions, government institutions and head offices of banks are closed for business. However, local bank branches are open for about 5 hours a day for 1 to 3 days. Shopping centers are open till mid-night while supermarkets and medium-sized shops keep normal opening hours. Local shops and convenience stores vary, some trading for fewer hours during the holidays.

January 1: New Year's Day   **Xīnnián/Yuándàn**   新年/元旦
[**Yīyuè yīhào**]

January/February: Chinese New Year   **Chūnjié**   春节
(Lunar Calendar: First Day of the First Month)
[**Nónglì Zhēngyuè yīrì**]

January/February: Lantern Festival   **Yuánxiāojié**   元宵节
(Lunar Calendar: Fifteenth Day of the First Month)
[**Nónglì Zhēngyuè shíwǔrì**]

March 8: Women's Day   **Fùnǚjié**   妇女节
[**Sānyuè bāhào**]

April 5: Festival of Sweeping Ancestors' Graves
[**Sìyuè wǔhào**]   **Qīngmíngjié**   清明节

May 1: Labor Day   **Láodòngjié**   劳动节
[**Wǔyuè yīhào**]

May 4: Youth Festival   **Qīngniánjié**   青年节
[**Wǔyuè sìhào**]

June 1: Children's Day   **Értóngjié**   儿童节
[**Liùyuè yīhào**]

June: Dragon Boat Festival   **Duānwǔjié**   端午节
(Lunar Calendar: Fifth Day of the Fifth Month)
[**Nónglì Wǔyuè wǔrì**]

July 1: Foundation Day of Chinese Communist Party
[**Qīyuè yīhào**]   **Jiàndǎngjié**   建党节

August 1: Foundation Day of the People's Liberation Army
[**Bāyuè yīhào**]   **Jiànjūnjié**   建军节

Mid-Autumn: Mid-Autumn Festival   **Zhōngqiūjié**   中秋节
[**Nónglì Bāyuè shíwǔrì**]

October 1: National Day   **Guóqìngjié**   国庆节
[**Shíyuè yīhào**]

Telephone alphabets

● **The phonological system of Mandarin Chinese**, Hanyu Pinyin, can be represented by letters. Twenty five letters of all the letters of English alphabet are used for Pinyin. Letter "**v**" is not used, while letter "**ü**" is added to represent the vowel sound "**yü**." Below is how Pinyin may sound like in terms of English pronunciation. All rules given here in terms of English pronunciation are approximations, as several of these sounds do not correspond directly to sounds in English.

Pinyin	English	Examples	(Meaning)
ao	now	到 **dào**	(arrive)
b	bee	白 **bái**	(white)
c	(i)ts	藏 **cáng**	(hide)
ch	ch	茶 **chá**	(tea)
d	day	地 **dì**	(earth)
e	her	这 **zhè**	(this)
ei	day	背 **bèi**	(the back)
er	err	儿 **ér**	(son)
f	far	饭 **fàn**	(meal)
g	good	狗 **gǒu**	(dog)
h	how	行 **háng**	(row)
i	eat	你 **nǐ**	(you)
ian	yen	电 **diàn**	(electricity)
ie	yes	裂 **liè**	(crack)
iu	you	丢 **diū**	(lose)
j	jeep	家 **jiā**	(home)
k	key	看 **kàn**	(see)
l	lay	蓝 **lán**	(blue)
m	my	米 **mǐ**	(uncooked rice)
n	nine	能 **néng**	(energy)
o	awe	破 **pò**	(broken)
ou	low	豆 **dòu**	(bean)

The Basics

1

p	pea	怕 **pà**	(scare)
q	cheer	请 **qǐng**	(please)
r	rat	人 **rén**	(people)
s	see	三 **sān**	(three)
sh	she	深 **shēn**	(deep)
t	tea	田 **tián**	(field)
u	wool	路 **lù**	(road)
ui	way	灰 **huī**	(grey)
uo	ward	拖 **tuō**	(drag)
ü	ü (French)	绿 **lǜ**	(green)
üe	ü + ebb	学 **xué**	(learn)
w	way	晚 **wǎn**	(late)
x	see	谢 **xiè**	(thank)
y	young	羊 **yáng**	(sheep)
z	kids	脏 **zāng**	(dirty)
zh	gauge	周 **zhōu**	(week)

2 Meet and Greet

2.1	Greetings	34
2.2	Asking a question	36
2.3	How to reply	38
2.4	Thank you	40
2.5	I'm sorry	41
2.6	What do you think?	41

2. Meet and Greet

● **It is normal** in China to shake hands on meeting and parting company. The strength of the handshake is determined by the level of acquaintance and the importance of the occasion. Generally one should refrain from giving a strong handshake to male or female acquaintances. Hugging is reserved for relatives and kissing on the cheeks is rarely seen among Chinese except perhaps on occasions involving expatriate communities.

2.1 Greetings

Hello/Good morning, Mr Williams	**Nǐ hǎo/Zǎo, Wēilín xiānsheng!** 你好／早, 威林先生！
Hello/Good morning, Mrs Jones	**Nǐ hǎo/Zǎo, Qióngsī tàitai/fūren!** 你好／早, 琼司太太／夫人！
Hello, Peter	**Nǐ hǎo, Bǐdé!** 你好，彼德！
Hi, Helen	**Nǐ hǎo, Kǎilún!** 你好，凯伦！
Good morning, madam	**Zǎoshang hǎo, tàitai/fūren!** 早上好，太太／夫人
Good afternoon, sir	**Xiàwǔ hǎo, xiānsheng!** 下午好，先生！
Good evening	**Nǐ hǎo/Wǎnshang hǎo!** 你好／晚上好！
Hello/Good morning	**Nǐ hǎo/Zǎoshang hǎo!** 你好／早上好！
How are you?/ How are things?	**Nǐ hǎo ma?/Zěnmeyàng?** 你好吗／怎么样？
Fine, thank you, and you?	**Hái hǎo, xièxie, nǐ ne?** 还好, 谢谢, 你呢？

Very well, and you?	**Hěn hǎo, nǐ ne?** 很好，你呢？
In excellent health/ In great shape	**Jīngshén hǎo/Shēntǐ hǎo** 精神好 / 身体好
So-so	**Mǎmǎhūhū/Hái xíng/Còuhé** 马马虎虎 / 还行 / 凑合
Not very well	**Bù zěnme hǎo** 不怎么好
Not bad	**Búcuò/Hái hǎo** 不错 / 还好
I'm going to leave	**Wǒ zǒu le** 我走了
I have to be going, someone's waiting for me	**Wǒ děi zǒu le, yǒu rén zài děng wǒ** 我得走了，有人在等我
Good-bye	**Zàijiàn!** 再见！
See you later	**Huítóu jiàn!/Yìhuǐr jiàn!** 回头见！ / 一会儿见！
See you soon	**Zàijiàn!** 再见！
See you in a little while!	**Dāi huǐr jiàn!** 待会儿见！
Sweet dreams!	**Zuò ge hǎo mèng!** 做个好梦
Good night!	**Wǎn'ān!** 晚安！
All the best/Good luck!	**Zhù nǐ hǎo yùn!** 祝你好运！
Have fun!	**Wánr kāixīn diǎnr!** 玩开心点儿！
Have a nice vacation!	**Jiàqī yúkuài!** 假期愉快！
Have a good weekend!	**Zhōumò yúkuài!** 周末愉快！

Bon voyage/ Have a good trip	**Yī lù píng'ān!/Lǚtú yúkuài!** 一路平安！/ 旅途愉快！
Thank you, the same to you	**Xièxie, nǐ yě yíyàng** 谢谢，你也一样
Say hello to/Give my regards to… (formal)	**Dài…wèn hǎo/Qǐng nǐ dài wǒ xiàng…wèn hǎo** 代…问好 / 请你代我向…问好
Say hello to… (informal)	**Xiàng…wèn hǎo** 向…问好

2.2 Asking a question

Who?	**Shéi?** 谁？
Who's that?/Who is it?/ Who's there?	**Shì shéi?/Nín shì shéi?/Shéi ya?** 是谁？/ 您是谁？/ 谁呀？
What?	**Shénme?** 什么？
What is there to see?	**Yǒu shénme hǎo kàn de?** 有什么好看的？
What category of hotel is it?	**Zhè jiā lǚguǎn shì jǐ xīng jí de?** 这家旅馆是几星级的？
Where?	**Nǎr/Nǎli?** 哪儿？/ 哪里？
Where's the bathroom?	**Cèsuǒ zài nǎr/nǎli?** 厕所在哪儿 / 哪里？
Where are you going?	**Nǐ shàng nǎr/nǎli qù?** 你上哪儿 / 哪里去？
Where are you from?	**Nǐ cóng nǎr/nǎli qù?** 你从哪儿 / 哪里来？
What?/How?	**Shénme?/Zěnme?** 什么 / 怎么？
What's your name? (formal)	**Nǐ guì xìng?/Zěnme chēnghū nín?** 您贵姓？/ 怎么称呼您？

What's your name? (informal)	**Nǐ jiào shénme míngzi?** 你叫什么名字？
How far is that?	**Yào duō yuǎn?** 要多远？
How long does that take?	**Yào duō jiǔ?/Yào duō cháng shíjiān?** 要多久？ / 要多长时间？
How long is the trip?	**Lùchéng yào duō jiǔ?/Lùchéng yào duō cháng shíjiān?** 路程要多久？ / 路程要多长时间？
How much?	**Duōshao qián?** 多少钱？
How much is this?	**Zhè (ge) duōshao qián?** 这（个）多少钱？
What time is it?	**Jǐ diǎn le?/Shénme shíhou le?** 几点了？ / 什么时候了？
Which one/s?	**Nǎ ge/ Nǎ xiē?** 哪个 / 哪些？
Which glass is mine?	**Nǎ ge bēizi shì wǒde?** 哪个杯子是我的？
When?	**Shénme shíhou?** 什么时候？
When are you leaving? (formal)	**Nǐ shénme shíhou chūfā?** 你什么时候出发？
Why?	**Wèishénme?** 为什么？
Could you...? (formal)	**Néng/kěyǐ...ma?/Kě bu kěyǐ...?/ Qǐng...** 能 / 可以…吗？ / 可不可以…？ / 请…
Could you help me/ give me a hand please?	**Nǐ néng/kěyǐ bāngzhu wǒ ma?** 你能 / 可以帮助我吗？
	Qǐng bāng wǒ ge máng 请帮我个忙
Could you point that out to me/show me please?	**Qǐng zhǐ gěi wǒ kàn** 请指给我看

Could you come with me, please?	**Qǐng gén wǒ lái** 请跟我来
Could you reserve/book me some tickets please?	**Qǐng gěi wǒ yùdǐng jǐ zhāng piào** 请给我预订几张票
Could you recommend another hotel?	**Qǐng gěi wǒ tuījiàn yī jiā lǚguǎn, hǎo ma?** 请给我推荐一家旅馆, 好吗?
Do you know...? (formal)	**Nǐ zhī bu zhīdao...?** 你知不知道…?
Do you know whether...?	**Nǐ zhī bu zhīdao shìfǒu...?** 你知不知道是否…?
Do you have...?	**Yǒu méiyǒu...?** 有没有…?
Do you have a vegetarian dish, please?	**Qǐngwèn, yǒu méiyǒu sùshí de cài/sùcài?** 请问, 有没有素食的菜 / 素菜?
I would like...	**Wǒ yào (yí ge)...** 我要(一个)…
I'd like a kilo of apples, please	**Qǐng gěi wǒ yī gōngjīn píngguǒ** 请给我一公斤苹果
Can/May I?	**Wǒ néng/kěyǐ...?** 我能 / 可以…?
Can/May I take this away?	**Wǒ néng/kěyǐ názǒu ma?** 我能 / 可以拿走吗?
Can I smoke here?	**Wǒ kěyǐ zài zhèlǐ chōuyān/xīyān ma?** 我可以在这里抽烟 / 吸烟吗?
Could I ask you something?	**Kěyǐ wèn nín jiàn shìr ma?** 可以问您件事儿吗?

2.3 How to reply

My name is ...	**Wǒ xìng.../Wǒ jiào....** 我姓 / 我叫…

Yes, of course	**Shì, dāngrán** 是，当然
No, I'm sorry	**Búshì, duìbuqǐ** 不是，对不起
Yes, what can I do for you?	**Duì, zhào wǒ yǒu shìr ma?** 对，找我有事儿吗？
Just a moment, please	**Qǐng děng yìhuǐr** 请等一会儿
No, I don't have time now	**Duìbuqǐ, wǒ xiànzài méiyǒu kòngr** 对不起，我现在没有空儿
No, that's impossible	**Duìbuqǐ, bànbudào** 对不起，办不到
I think so/I think that's absolutely right	**Wǒ kàn shì zhèyàng/Wǒ xiǎng juéduì méi wèntí** 我看是这样／我想绝对没问题
I think so too/I agree	**Wǒ yě juéde shì zhèyàng/Wǒ tóngyì** 我也觉得是这样／我同意
I hope so too	**Wǒ yě dànyuàn shì zhèyàng** 我也但愿是这样
No, not at all/ Absolutely not	**Bù, búshì zhèyàng/Juéduì búshì** 不，不是这样／绝对不是
No, no one	**Méiyǒu, méiyǒu rén** 没有，没有人
No, nothing	**Bù, méiyǒu** 不，没有
That's right	**Duì!** 对！
Something's wrong	**Chūshì le/Chū wèntí le** 出事了／出问题了
I agree (don't agree)	**Wǒ tóngyì (Wǒ bù tóngyì)** 我同意（我不同意）
OK/it's fine	**Hǎo, méiyǒu wèntí** 好，没有问题

OK, all right	**Hǎo, jiù zhèyàng** 好，就这样
Perhaps/maybe	**Yěxǔ/Kěnéng** 也许／可能
I don't know	**Wǒ bù zhīdao** 我不知道

2.4 Thank you

Thank you	**Xièxie** 谢谢！
You're welcome	**Bú kèqi** 不客气
Thank you very much/ Many thanks	**Gǎnxiè gǎnxiè/Fēicháng gǎnxiè** 感谢感谢／非常感谢
Very kind of you	**Nín tài kèqi le** 您太客气了
My pleasure	**Bié kèqi/Wǒde róngxìng** 别客气／我的荣幸
I enjoyed it very much	**Wǒ fēicháng xǐhuan** 我非常喜欢
Thank you for...	**Xièxie nǐ gěi wǒ...** 谢谢你给我…
You shouldn't have/ That was so kind of you	**Nǐ bù gāi zhèyàng kèqi/Nǐ tài kèqi le** 你不该这样客气／您太客气了
Don't mention it!	**Búyòng xiè!** 不用谢
That's all right	**Bú kèqi** 不客气

2.5 I'm sorry

Excuse me/pardon me/ sorry (formal)	**Láojià/Bàoqiàn/Duìbuqǐ/Bùhǎoyìsī** 劳驾 / 抱歉 / 对不起 / 不好意思
Excuse me/pardon me/ sorry (informal)	**Qǐng wèn yīxià/Duìbuqǐ/Máfan nǐ le** 请问一下 / 对不起 / 麻烦你了
Sorry, I didn't know that...	**Duìbuqǐ, wǒ bù zhīdao ...** 对不起，我不知道…
Excuse/pardon me (formal)	**Láojià/Qǐngwèn** 劳驾 / 请问
I do apologize (formal/informal)	**Wǒ zhēnchéng dàoqiàn/Tài duìbuqǐ le** 我真诚道歉 / 太对不起了
I'm sorry	**Duìbuqǐ** 对不起
I didn't mean it/ It was an accident	**Wǒ búshì gùyì de/Zhè shì ge yìwài** 我不是故意的 / 这是个意外
That's all right/Don't worry about it (formal)	**Bú yàojǐn/Méi guānxi** 不要紧 / 没关系
Never mind/Forget it (informal)	**Bú ài'shì/Méi shì** 不碍事 / 没事
It could happen to anyone	**Shéi yě miǎnbuliǎo** 谁也免不了

2.6 What do you think?

Which do you prefer?/ like best? (formal)	**Nǐ xǐhuan nǎ ge?/Nǐ zuì xǐhuan nǎ ge?** 你喜欢哪个？/ 你最喜欢哪个？
What do you think? (informal)	**Nǐ juéde zěnmeyàng?/Nǐ kàn zěnmeyàng?** 你觉得怎么样？/ 你看怎么样？
Don't you like dancing?	**Nǐ bù xǐhuan tiàowǔ ma?** 你不喜欢跳舞吗？
I don't mind	**Wǒ wúsuǒwèi** 我无所谓

Well done!	**Tài bàng le!** 太棒了！
Not bad!	**Búcuò!** 不错！
Great!/Marvelous!	**Hǎojíle!** 好极了！
Wonderful!	**Tài hǎo le!** 太好了！
How lovely!	**Tài měi le!** 太美了！
I am pleased for you (formal/informal)	**Wǒ wèi nǐ gāoxìng/Wǒ tì nǐ gāoxìng** 我为你高兴 / 我替你高兴
I'm very happy/ delighted to...	**....wǒ hěn gāoxìng** …我很高兴
It's really nice here!	**Zhèlǐ jiǎnzhí tài hǎo le!** 这里简直太好了！
How nice!/How nice for you!	**Zhēn hǎo!** 真好！
I'm (not) very happy with...	**Wǒ duì...hěn mǎnyì/Wǒ duì...bù mǎnyì** 我对…很满意 / 我对…不满意
I'm glad that....	**Wǒ wèi...gāoxìng** 我为…高兴
I'm having a great time	**Wǒ wánrde hěn gāoxìng** 我玩儿得很高兴
I can't wait till tomorrow	**Wǒ kě děngbudào míngtiān la** 我可等不到明天啦
I'm looking forward to tomorrow	**Wǒ qīdàizhe míngtiān de láilín** 我期待着明天的来临
I hope it works out	**Wǒ xīwàng yíqiè jìnxíng shùnlì** 我希望一切进行顺利
How awful!	**Tài zāogāo le!** 太糟糕了！
It's horrible	**Tài kǒngbù le!** 太恐怖了！

That's ridiculous!	**Tài kěxiào le!**
	太可笑了！
That's terrible!	**Tài kěpà le!**
	太可怕了！
What a pity/shame!	**Zhēn kěxī!**
	真可惜！
How disgusting!	**Zhēn èxīn!**
	真恶心！
What nonsense/	**Shuō shénme fèihuà!/Zhēn shì hú'nào!**
How silly!	说什么废话！／真是胡闹！
I don't like it/them	**Wǒ bù xǐhuan/Wǒ bù xǐhuan tāmen**
	我不喜欢／我不喜欢他们
I'm bored to death	**Mènsǐ le**
	闷死了！
I'm fed up	**Fánsǐ rén le**
	烦死人了！
This is no good	**Zhè kě bù hǎo**
	这可不好
This is not what I	**Wǒ kě méi xiǎngdào huì zhèyàng**
expected	我可没想到会这样

3 Small Talk

3.1	Introductions	45
3.2	I beg your pardon?	49
3.3	Starting/ending a conversation	50
3.4	A chat about the weather	51
3.5	Hobbies	51
3.6	Invitations	52
3.7	Paying a compliment	54
3.8	Intimate comments/questions	55
3.9	Congratulations and condolences	56
3.10	Arrangements	57
3.11	Being the host(ess)	57
3.12	Saying good-bye	58

3. Small Talk

3.1 Introductions

May I introduce myself?	**Zìwǒ jièshào yí xià** 自我介绍一下
My name's...	**Wǒ jiào...** 我叫…
I'm...	**Wǒ shì...** 我是
What's your name? (formal)	**Qǐngwèn, nín guìxìng?** 请问，您贵姓？
What's your name? (informal)	**Nǐ jiào shénme míngzi?** 你叫什么名字？
May I introduce...?	**Wǒ lài jièshào, zhè shì..., zhè shì...** 我来介绍，这是…，这是…
This is my wife/husband	**Zhè shì wǒ qīzi/zhàngfu** 这是我妻子／丈夫
This is my daughter/son	**Zhè shì wǒ nǚ'ér/érzi** 这是我女儿／儿子
This is my mother/ father (formal)	**Zhè shì wǒ mǔqin/fùqin** 这是我母亲／父亲
This is my mother/ father (informal)	**Zhè shì wǒ mā/wǒ bà** 这是我妈／我爸
This is my fiancée/fiancé	**Zhè shì wǒ wèihūnqī/wèihūnfū** 这是我未婚妻／未婚夫
This is my girlfriend/ boyfriend	**Zhè shì wǒ nǚpéngyou/nánpéngyou** 这是女朋友／男朋友
This is my friend	**Zhè shì wǒ péngyou** 这是我朋友
How do you do?	**Nǐ hǎo!** 你好！

Hi, pleased to meet you (informal)	**Nǐ hǎo, rènshi nǐ hěn gāoxìng** 你好, 认识你很高兴
Pleased to meet you (formal)	**Xìnghuì, xìnghuì!/Rènshi nǐ hěn gāoxìng** 幸会, 幸会! / 认识你很高兴
Where are you from? (formal/informal)	**Nǐ shì nǎguórén?/Nǐ cóng nǎli lái?** 你是哪国人? / 你从哪里来?
I'm American/British/ Candadian/Australian/ Japanese	**Wǒ shì Měiguórén/Yīngguórén/ Jiānádàrén/Àodàlìyàrén/Rìběnrén** 我是美国人 / 英国人/加拿大人/ 澳大利亚人 / 日本人
What city do you live in?	**Nǐ zhù zài nǎ ge chéngshì?** 你住在哪个城市?
In.../near...	**Zài.../Kàojìn...** 在… / 靠近…
Have you been here long?	**Nǐ lái zhèlǐ duō jiǔ le?** 你来这里多久了?
A few days	**Zhǐ yǒu jǐ tiān** 只有几天
How long are you staying here?	**Nǐ yào zài zhèr zhù duō jiǔ?** 你要在这儿住多久?
We'll (probably) be leaving tomorrow	**Wǒmen (kěnéng) míngtiān zǒu** 我们(可能)明天走
We'll (probably) be leaving in two weeks	**Wǒmen (kěnéng) liǎng ge xīngqī zǒu** 我们(可能)两个星期走
Where are you staying?	**Nǐ zhù zài nǎr?** 你住在哪儿?
I'm staying in a hotel	**Wǒ zhù zài yì jiā lǚguǎn** 我住在一家旅馆
I'm staying with friends/ relatives	**Wǒ zhù zài péngyou/qīnqi jiā** 我住在朋友 / 亲戚家
Are you here on your own?/Are you here with your family?	**Nǐ yí ge rén lái ma?/Nǐ gēn jiārén lái ma?** 你一个人来吗? / 你跟家人来吗?

I'm on my own | **Wǒ yí ge rén lái**
我一个人来

I'm with my wife/ husband | **Wǒ gēn wǒ qīzi/zhàngfu lái**
我跟我妻子／丈夫来

– with my family | **Wǒ gēn jiārén lái**
我跟家人来

– with relatives | **Wǒ gēn qīnqi lái**
我跟亲戚来

– with a friend/friends | **Wǒ gēn péngyou lái**
我跟朋友来

Are you married? | **Nǐ jiéhūn le méiyǒu?**
你结婚了没有？

Do you have a steady boyfriend/girlfriend? | **Nǐ yǒu nánpéngyou/nǔpéngyou méiyǒu?**
你有男朋友／女朋友没有？

I'm married | **Wǒ jiéhūn le**
我结婚了

I'm single | **Wǒ dānshēn**
我单身

I'm not married | **Wǒ méi jiéhūn**
我没结婚

I'm separate | **Wǒ gēn wǒ qīzi/zhàngfu fēnjū le**
我跟我妻子／丈夫分居了

I'm divorced | **Wǒ líhūn le**
我离婚了

I'm a widow/widower | **Wǒ de zhàngfu/qīzi qùshì le**
我的丈夫／妻子去世了

I live alone | **Wǒ yí ge rén zhù**
我一个人住

Do you have any children/grandchildren? | **Nǐ yǒu méiyǒu háizi/sūnzi?**
你有没有孩子／孙子？

How old are you? (addressing young people) | **Nǐ duō dà le?**
你多大了？

(informal way of addressing older people)	**Nín jīnnián duō dà le?** 您今年多大了？
(formal way of addressing older people)	**Nín duō dà suìshù/niānjì le?** 您多大岁数／年纪了？
How old is she/he?	**Tā duō dà le?** 她／他多大了？
I'm...(years old)	**Wǒ jīnnián...suì** 我今年…岁
She's/He's...(years old)	**Tā jīnnián...suì** 她／他今年…岁
What do you do for a living? (formal/informal)	**Nǐ zuò shénme gōngzuò?** 你做什么工作？
	Nǐ shì zuò shénme de? 你是做什么的？
I work in an office	**Wǒ zài bàn gōngshì gōngzuò** 我在办公室工作
I'm a student	**Wǒ shì xuésheng** 我是学生
I'm unemployed	**Wǒ shìyè le** 我失业了
I'm retired	**Wǒ tuìxiū le** 我退休了
I'm on a disability pension	**Wǒ zài lǐng shāngcán fǔxùjīn** 我在领伤残抚恤金
I'm a housewife	**Wǒ shì jiātíng fùnǚ** 我是家庭妇女
Do you like your job?	**Nǐ xǐhuan nǐde gōngzuò ma?** 你喜欢你的工作吗？
Most of the time	**Dà duō shíhou xǐhuan** 大多时候喜欢
Mostly I do, but I prefer vacations	**Wǒ xǐhuan wǒde gōngzuò, búguò wǒ gèng xǐhuan fàngjià** 我喜欢我的工作，不过我更喜欢放假

I don't speak any/
I speak a little...
**Wǒ bú huì shuō.../Wǒ huì shuō
yìdiǎn...**
我不会说… / 我会说一点…

I'm American/British/
Candadian/Australian/
Japanese
**Wǒ shì Měiguórén/Yīngguórén/
Jiānádàrén/Àodàlìyàrén/Rìběnrén**
我是美国人 / 英国人/加拿大人/
澳大利亚人 / 日本人

Do you speak English?
(formal)
Nǐ huì shuō Yīngyǔ/Yīngwén ma?
你会说英语 / 英文吗？

Is there anyone
who speaks...?
Zhèlǐ yǒu méiyǒu rén huì shuō...?
这里有没有人会说…？

I beg your pardon/What?
Shénme?
什么

I (don't) understand
Wǒ (bù) dǒng
我（不）懂

Do you understand me?
(formal)
Nǐ dǒng wǒ shuō de huà ma?
你懂我说的话吗？

Could you repeat that,
please?
Qǐng nǐ zài shuō yí biàn
请你再说一遍

Could you speak more
slowly, please?
Qǐng nǐ shuō màn yìdiǎn
请你说慢一点

What does this/
that mean?
Zhè/Nà shì shénme yìsi?
这 / 那是什么意思？

It's more or less the
same as...
Zhè gēn...chàbuduō yíyàng
这跟…差不多一样

Could you write that
down for me, please?
Qǐng gěi wǒ xiěxiàlai
请给我写下来

Could you spell that
for me, please?
Qǐng yòng zìmǔ pīnchūlai
请用字母拼出来

Could you point to the
phrase in this book,
please?
**Qǐng zài zhè běn shū lǐ zhǐchū zhè
jù huà**
请在这本书里指出这句话

Just a minute, I'll look it up	**Qǐng děngyiděng, wǒ chácha** 请等一等，我查查
I can't find the word/ sentence	**Wǒ zhǎobudào zhè ge cí/jùzi** 我找不到这个词／句子
How do you say that in...?	**...zěnme shuō** …怎么说？
How do you pronounce that word?	**Zhè ge cí zěnme niàn?** 这个词怎么念？

3.3 Starting/ending a conversation

Could I ask you something?	**Wǒ kěyǐ wèn nǐ yí jiàn shì ma?** 我可以问你一件事吗？
Excuse/Pardon me (formal/informal)	**Láojià/Bàoqiàn, Qǐngwèn/Duìbuqǐ** 劳驾／抱歉，请问／对不起
Could you help me please?	**Kěyǐ bāng ge máng ma?** 可以帮个忙吗？
Yes, what's the problem?	**Kěyǐ, yǒu shénme shì?** 可以，有什么事？
What can I do for you?	**Yǒu shénme wǒ kěyǐ bāng nǐ de?** 有什么我可以帮你的？
Sorry, I don't have time now	**Duìbuqǐ wǒ xiànzài méi kòngr** 对不起，我现在没空儿
Do you have a light?	**Yǒu méiyǒu dǎhuǒjī/huǒchái?** 有没有打火机／火柴？
May I join you?	**Wǒ kěyǐ jiārù (nǐmen) ma?** 我可以加入（你们）吗？
Can I take a picture?	**Wǒ kěyǐ zhào zhāng xiàng ma?** 我可以照张相吗？
Could you take a picture of me/us?	**Nǐ kěyǐ gěi wǒ/wǒmen zhào zhāng xiàng ma?** 你可以给我／我们照张相吗？
Leave me alone	**Bié chán wǒ/Ràng wǒ jìng yíxià** 别缠我／让我静一下

Get lost	**Zǒukāi!**
	走开！
Go away or I'll scream	**Nǐ zài bù zǒukāi wǒ jiù dàshēng hǎn le**
	你再不走开我就大声喊了

3.4 A chat about the weather

See also 1.5 The weather

It's so hot/cold today!	**Jīntiān zhēn rè/lěng!**
	今天真热 / 冷！
Isn't it a lovely day?	**Jīntiān tiānqì tài hǎo le!**
	今天天气太好了！
It's so windy/what a storm!	**Fēng tài dà le/Guā dàfēng le**
	风太大了 / 刮大风了
All that rain/snow!	**Xià zhème dà de yǔ/xuě!**
	下这么大的雨 / 雪！
It's so foggy!	**Xià zhème dà de wù!**
	下这么大的雾！
Has the weather been like this for long?	**Zhèyàng de tiānqì hěn jiǔ le ma?**
	这样的天气很久了吗？
Is it always this hot/cold here?	**Zhèlǐ zǒngshì zhème rè/lěng ma?**
	这里总是这么热 / 冷吗？
Is it always this dry/humid here?	**Zhèlǐ zǒngshì zhème gānzào/cháoshī ma?**
	这里总是这么干燥 / 潮湿吗？

3.5 Hobbies

Do you have any hobbies?	**Nǐ yǒu shénme àihào?**
	你有什么爱好？
I like knitting/reading/photography	**Wǒ xǐhuan dǎ máoyī/kànshū/shèyǐng**
	我喜欢打毛衣 / 看书 / 摄影

I enjoy listening to music	**Wǒ xǐhuan tīng yīnyuè** 我喜欢听音乐
I play the guitar/piano	**Wǒ xǐhuan tán jítā/gāngqín** 我喜欢弹吉他 / 钢琴
I like the cinema	**Wǒ xǐhuan kàn diànyǐng** 我喜欢看电影
I like traveling/playing sports/going fishing/going for a walk	**Wǒ xǐhuan qù lǚyóu/yùndòng/ diàoyú/qù sànbù** 我喜欢去旅游 / 运动 / 钓鱼 / 去散步

3.6 Invitations

Are you doing anything tonight?	(formal) **Wǎnshang yǒu shénme huódòng?** 晚上有什么活动？
	(informal) **Wǎnshang nǐ xiǎng zuò shénme?** 晚上你想做什么？
Do you have any plans for today/this afternoon/tonight?	(formal) **Jīntiān/Xiàwǔ/Wǎnshang yǒu shénme huódòng?** 今天 / 下午 / 晚上有什么活动？
	(informal) **Jīntiān/Xiàwǔ/Wǎnshang yǒu shénme ānpái?** 今天 / 下午 / 晚上有什么安排？
Would you like to go out with me?	(formal) **Nǐ xiǎng gēn wǒ wàichū ma?** 你想跟我外出吗？
	(informal) **Gēn wǒ chūqu wánr, zěnmeyàng?** 跟我出去玩儿，怎么样？
Would you like to go dancing with me?	(formal) **Nǐ xiǎng gēn wǒ qù tiàowǔ ma?** 你想跟我去跳舞吗？
	(informal) **Gēn wǒ qù tiàowǔ, zěnmeyàng?** 跟我去跳舞，怎么样？

Would you like to have lunch/dinner with me?	(formal) **Nǐ xiǎng gēn wǒ qù chī wǔfàn/wǎnfàn ma?** 你想跟我去吃午饭／晚饭吗？
	(informal) **Gēn wǒ qù chī wǔfàn/wǎnfàn, zěnmeyàng?** 跟我去吃午饭／晚饭，怎么样？
Would you like to come to the beach with me?	(formal) **Nǐ xiǎng gēn wǒ qù hǎitān ma?** 你想跟我去海滩吗？
	(informal) **Gēn wǒ qù hǎitān, zěnmeyàng?** 跟我去海滩，怎么样？
Would you like to come into town with us?	(formal) **Nǐ xiǎng gēn wǒmen jìnchéng ma?** 你想跟我们进城吗？
	(informal) **Gēn wǒmen jìnchéng, zěnmeyàng?** 跟我们进城，怎么样？
Would you like to come and see some friends with us?	(formal) **Nǐ xiǎng gēn wǒmen qù kàn péngyou ma?** 你想跟我们去看朋友吗？
	(informal) **Gēn wǒmen qù kàn péngyou, zěnmeyàng?** 跟我们去看朋友，怎么样？
Shall we dance?	**Tiàowǔ ma?** 跳舞吗？
– sit at the bar?	**Qù jiǔbā zuòzuo?** 去酒吧坐坐？
– get something to drink?	**Hē diǎn shénme yǐnliào?** 喝点什么饮料？
– go for a walk/drive?	**Chūqu zǒuzou/Kāichē guàngyiguàng?** 出去走走／开车逛一逛？
Yes, all right	**Hǎo a!** 好啊！

Good idea	**Hǎo zhǔyì!**
	好主意！
No thank you	**Bùle, xièxie**
	不了，谢谢
Maybe later	**Wǎn diǎnr ba**
	晚点儿吧
I don't feel like it	**Wǒ méiyǒu xìngqù**
	我没有兴趣
I don't have time	**Wǒ méiyǒu kòngr**
	我没有空儿
I already have a date	**Wǒ yǐjīng yǒu yuēhuì le**
	我已经有约会了
I'm not very good at dancing/swimming	**Wǒ tiào/yóu de bú tài hǎo**
	我跳／游得不太好

3.7 Paying a compliment

You look great! (formal/informal)	**Nǐ kàn shàngqu zhēn shuài!**
	你看上去真帅！
	Jǐntiān zěnme zhème shuài!
	今天怎么这么帅！
I like your car!	**Nǐ de chē zhēn hǎokàn!/Wǒ xǐhuan nǐde chē!**
	你的车真好看！／我喜欢你的车！
You are very nice (formal/informal)	**Nǐ (duǐ) rén zhēn hǎo!/Nǐ zhēn hǎo!**
	你（对）人真好！／你真好！
What a good boy/girl!	**Hǎo háizi!**
	好孩子！
You're a good dancer	**Nǐ tiàowǔ tiàode hěn hǎo**
	你跳舞跳得很好
You're a very good cook	**Nǐ zuòcài zuòde hěn hǎo**
	你做菜做得很好
You're a good soccer player	**Nǐ zúqiú tīde hěn hǎo**
	你足球踢得很好

I like being with you — **Wǒ xǐhuan gēn nǐ zài yìqǐ**
我喜欢跟你在一起

I've missed you so much — **Wǒ fēicháng xiǎngniàn nǐ**
我非常想念你

I dreamt about you — **Wǒ mèngjiàn nǐ**
我梦见你

I think about you all day — **Wǒ yìtiān-dàowǎn dōu xiǎngzhe nǐ**
我一天到晚都想着你

I've been thinking about you all day — **Wǒ zhěngtiān dōu zài xiǎng nǐ**
我整天都在想你

You have such a sweet smile — **Nǐde xiàoróng zhēn tián**
你的笑容真甜

You have such beautiful eyes — **Nǐde yǎnjing duōme mírén**
你的眼睛多么迷人

I love you (I'm fond of you) — **Wǒ xǐhuanshàng nǐ le**
我喜欢上你了

I'm in love with you — **Wǒ àishàng nǐ le**
我爱上你了

I'm in love with you too — **Wǒ yě àishàng nǐ le**
我也爱上你了

I love you — **Wǒ ài nǐ**
我爱你

I love you too — **Wǒ yě ài nǐ**
我也爱你

I don't feel as strongly about you — **Wǒ duì nǐ méiyǒu tèbié de gǎnqíng**
我对你没有特别的感情

I already have a girlfriend/boyfriend — **Wǒ yǐjīng yǒu nǚpéngyou/ nánpéngyou le**
我已经有女朋友／男朋友了

I'm not ready for that — **Wǒde gǎnqíng hái méiyǒu dào zhé yí bù**
我的感情还没有到这一步

I don't want to rush into it	**Wǒ bù xiǎng zhème kuài jiù xiànjìnqu** 我不想这么快就陷进去
Take your hands off me	**Bǎ nǐde shǒu nákāi!** 把你的手拿开！
Okay, no problem	**Hǎo, méi wèntí** 好，没问题
Will you spend the night with me?	**Nǐ yuànbuyuàn péi wǒ yì wǎn?** 你愿不愿陪我一晚？
I'd like to go to bed with you	**Wǒ xiǎng gēn nǐ shuìjiào** 我想跟你睡觉
Only if we use a condom	**Hǎo, búguò wǒmen yídìng yào yòng bìyùntào** 好，不过我们一定要用避孕套
We have to be careful about AIDS	**Wǒmen yào dāngxīn àizībìng** 我们要当心爱滋病
We shouldn't take any risks	**Wǒmen bù yīnggāi mào zhè ge xiǎn** 我们不应该冒这个险
Do you have a condom?	**Nǐ yǒu bìyùntào ma?** 你有避孕套吗？
No? Then the answer's no	**Méiyǒu? Nàme wǒ zhǐ néng shuō bù** 没有？那么我只能说不

3.9 Congratulations and condolences

Happy New Year	**(Zhù nǐ) xīnnián kuàilè!** （祝你）新年快乐！
Happy birthday	**(Zhù nǐ) shēngrì kuàilè!** （祝你）生日快乐！
Many happy returns	**(Zhù nǐ) shēngrì kuàilè!** （祝你）生日快乐！
Please accept my condolences	**Qǐng jiēshòu wǒde diàowèi** 请接受我的吊慰
My deepest sympathy	**Wǒ shēn yǒu tónggǎn** 我深有同感

3.10 Arrangements

When will I see you again?
Wǒmen shénme shíhou zài jiànmiàn?
我们什么时候再见面?

Are you free over the weekend?
Nǐ zhè ge zhǒumò yǒu méiyǒu kòngr?
你这个周末有没有空儿?

What's the plan, then?
Nǐ yǒu shénme ānpái?
你有什么安排?

Where shall we meet?
Wǒmen zài nǎr jiànmiàn?
我们在哪儿见面?

Will you pick me/us up?
Nǐ kěyǐ lái jiē wǒ/wǒmen ma?
你可以来接我／我们吗?

Shall I pick you up? (formal)
Wǒ lái jiē nǐ/nǐmen, hǎo bu hǎo?
我来接你／你们, 好不好?

I have to be home by...
Wǒ...yǐqián yídìng yào huídào jiālǐ
我…以前一定要回到家里

I don't want to see you anymore (formal)
Wǒ bù xiǎng zài jiàndào nǐ
我不想再见到你

3.11 Being the host(ess)

See also 4 Eating out

What would you like to drink?
(formal) **Nín xiǎng hē shénme yǐnliào?**
您想喝什么饮料?

(informal) **Xiǎng hē diǎn shénme?**
想喝点什么?

Something non-alcoholic, please
Yǒu méiyǒu bù hán jiǔjīng de yǐnliào?
有没有不含酒精的饮料?

Would you like a cigarette/cigar?
Xiǎng chōu zhī yān/xuějiā ma?
想抽只烟／雪茄吗?

I don't smoke
(Xièxie) wǒ bù chōuyān
(谢谢), 我不抽烟

Can I take you home? (formal)	**Wǒ kěyǐ sòng nǐ huíjiā ma?** 我可以送你回家吗？
Can I write/call you? (formal)	**Wǒ kěyǐ gěi nǐ xiěxìn/dǎ diànhuà ma?** 我可以给你写信／打电话吗？
Will you email me/ call me?	**Nǐ kěyǐ gěi wǒ fā diànzǐ yóujiàn/ dǎ diànhuà ma?** 你可以给我发电子邮件／打电话吗？
Can I have your address/ email address?	**Wǒ kěyǐ yào nǐde dǐzhǐ/diànzǐ yóujiàn dìzhǐ ma?** 我可以要你的地址／电子邮件地址吗？
Thanks for everything	**Gǎnxiè nǐ wèi wǒ zuò de yíqiè** 感谢你为我做的一切
It was a lot of fun	**Wánrde hěn kāixīn** 玩儿得很开心
Send my regards to… (informal)	**Qǐng dài wǒ gēn...wènhòu** 请代我跟⋯问候
All the best	**Wànshì-rúyì!** 万事如意！
Good luck	**Zhù nǐ hǎo yùn** 祝你好运
When will you be back? (informal)	**Nǐ shénme shíhou huílai?** 你什么时候回来？
I'll be waiting for you	**Wǒ huì děng nǐ huílai** 我会等你回来
I'd like to see you again	**Wǒ xiǎng zài jiàndào nǐ** 我想再见到你
I hope we meet again soon	**Wǒ xiǎng hěn kuài zài jiàndào nǐ** 我想很快再见到你
Here's my address if you're ever in the United States	**Zhè shì wǒde dìzhǐ. Yǒu yìtiān nǐ dào Měiguó lái, yídìng yào lái zhǎo wǒ** 这是我的地址。有一天你到美国来，一定要来找我

4 Eating Out

4.1	At the restaurant	60
4.2	Ordering	62
4.3	The bill	66
4.4	Complaints	67
4.5	Paying a compliment	68
4.6	Requests	68
4.7	Drinks	69
4.8	The menu	70

4. Eating Out

● **Foreigners visiting China** have a wide range of cuisines to choose from, such as Beijing Duck, Sichuan steamboat, Mongolian barbecues, Shanghai dumplings etc. In order to eat at most restaurants outside the hotels, it is sometimes necessary to make arrangements ahead of time. Most restaurants provide Chinese tea free of charge.

In China people usually have three meals:

1. **zǎofàn 早饭** (breakfast), is eaten sometime between 7.30 and 10 a.m. It generally consists of buns, congee, eggs, assorted pickles and noodles.

2. **wǔfàn 午饭** (lunch), traditionally eaten at home between 12 noon and 2 p.m., may include a hot dish. Schoolchildren return home at lunchtime, others bring along their packed lunch. Lunch usually consists of rice, a main course of meat or fish with a range of vegetable dishes, or noodles with meat and vegetables.

3. **wǎnfàn 晚饭** (dinner) is considered to be the most important meal of the day, at around 7 or 8 p.m. It often includes rice, a soup and a few meat and vegetable dishes, and is usually taken with the family.

4.1 At the restaurant

I'd like to reserve a table for seven o'clock, please	**Wǒ xiǎng dìng yì zhāng zhuō, dìng zài qīdiǎn** 我想订一张桌, 订在七点
A table for two, please	**Wǒ xiǎng dìng yì zhāng liǎng ge rén de zhuō** 我想订一张两个人的桌
We've reserved	**Wǒmen yùdìng le** 我们预订了
We haven't reserved	**Wǒmen hái méi yùdìng** 我们还没预订

请稍等！
Qǐng shāo děng!

A moment, please.

你预订座位了没有？
Nǐ yùdìng zuòwèile méiyǒu?

Do you have a reservation?

你们用谁的名字预订的？
Nǐmen yòng shuí de míngzi yùdìng de?

What name please?

这边请
Zhè biān qǐng

This way, please

（对不起），这张桌子已经预订了
(Duìbuqǐ), zhè zhāng zhuō yǐjīng yùdìngle

This table is reserved

十五分钟以后有一张空桌子
Shíwǔ fēnzhōng yǐhòu yǒuyì zhāng kōng zhuōzi

We'll have a table free in fifteen minutes

Would you mind waiting?

Nǐ jiè bu jiéyí děngyiděng?
你介不介意等一等？

Is the restaurant open yet?

Cāntīng kāimén le méiyǒu?
餐厅开门了没有？

What time does the restaurant open?

Cāntīng shénme shíhou kāimén?
餐厅什么时候开门？

What time does the restaurant close?

Cāntīng shénme shíhou guānmén?
餐厅什么时候关门？

Can we wait for a table?

Yàoshi/Rùguǒ wǒmen děng yíxià, yǒu méiyǒu zhuōzi?
要是／如果我们等一下，有没有桌子？

Do we have to wait long?

Wǒmen děi děng hěn jiǔ ma?
我们得等很久吗？

Is this seat taken?

Zhè ge wèizi yǒurén zuò ma?
这个位子有人坐吗？

Could we sit here/there?

Wǒmen kěyǐ zuò zài zhèr/nàr ma?
我们可以坐在这儿／那儿吗？

Can we sit by the window?

Wǒmen kěyǐ kào chuānghu zuò ma?
我们可以靠窗户坐吗？

Are there any tables outside?	**Wàibiān yǒu méiyǒu kōng zhuōzi?** 外边有没有空桌子？
Do you have another chair for us?	**Gěi wǒmen zài ná yì bǎ yǐzi, hǎo ma?** 给我们再拿一把椅子，好吗？
Do you have a high chair?	**Yǒu méiyǒu gěi xiǎo háizi zuò de gāo yǐzi?** 有没有给小孩子坐的高椅子？
Is there a socket for this bottle-warmer?	**Yǒu méiyǒu chā zhè ge nuǎnpíngqì de chāzuó?** 有没有插这个暖瓶器的插座？
Could you warm up this bottle/jar (in the microwave) for me?	**Qǐng gěi wǒ (zài wéibōlú lǐ) nuǎn yíxià zhè ge nǎipíng/dàkǒupíng** 请给我（在微波炉里）暖一下这个奶瓶／大口瓶
Not too hot, please	**Qǐng búyào tài tàng** 请不要太烫
Is there somewhere I can change the baby's diaper?	**Yǒu méiyǒu dìfang gěi yǐng'ér huàn niàobù?** 有没有地方给婴儿换尿布？
Where are the restrooms?	**Cèsuǒ zài nǎr/nǎli?** 厕所在哪儿／哪里？

4.2 Ordering

Waiter/Waitress!	**Fúwù yuán!** 服务员！
Madam!	**Nǚshì!** 女士！
Sir!	**Xiānsheng!** 先生！
We'd like something to eat/drink	**Wǒmen xiǎng chī/hē diǎn dōngxi** 我们想吃／喝点东西
Could I have a quick meal?	**Yǒu méiyǒu kuàicān?** 有没有快餐？

We don't have much time	**Wǒmen shíjiān bù duō** 我们时间不多
We'd like to have a drink first	**Wǒmen xiǎng xiān hē yǐnliào** 我们想先喝饮料
Could we see the menu/ wine list, please?	**Qǐng gěi wǒmen kànkan càidān/jiǔdān** 请给我们看看菜单／酒单
Do you have a menu in English?	**Yǒu méiyǒu Yīngwén de càidān** 有没有英文的菜单？
Do you have a dish of the day?	**Jīntiān yǒu méiyǒu tèbié de cài?** 今天有没有特别的菜？
Do you have a tourist menu?	**Yǒu méiyǒu zhuānmén gěi lǚkè yòng de càidān?** 有没有专门给旅客用的菜单？
We haven't made a choice yet	**Wǒmen hái méi xiǎnghǎo jiào shénme cài** 我们还没想好叫什么菜
What do you recommend?	**Nǐ kěyǐ gěi wǒmen jièshào jǐ dào cài ma?** 你可以给我们介绍几道菜吗？
What are the local specialities?	**Nǐmen běndì yǒu shénme fēngwēicài?** 你们本地有什么风味菜？
What are your specialities?	**Nǐmen fàn'guǎn tuījiàn shénme tèbié de cài?** 你们饭馆推荐什么特别的菜？
I like chilli/preserved vegetables	**Wǒ xǐhuan làjiāo/pàocài** 我喜欢辣椒／泡菜
I don't like meat/fish	**Wǒ bù xǐhuan chī ròu/yú** 我不喜欢吃肉／鱼
What's this?	**Zhè shì shénme?** 这是什么？
Does it have...in it?	**Lǐmiàn yǒu méiyǒu...?** 里面有没有…？
Is it stuffed with...?	**Lǐmiàn bāo de shìbushì...?** 里面包的是不是…？

What does it taste like?	**Chīqǐlai shénme wèi?** 吃起来什么味？
Is this a hot or cold dish?	**Zhè dào cài shì rè de háishi liáng de?** 这道菜是热的还是凉的？
Is this sweet?	**Zhè ge tián ma?** 这个甜吗？
Is this hot/spicy?	**Zhè ge là ma?** 这个辣吗？
	Zhè ge dài xiāngliào ma? 这个带香料吗？
Do you have anything else, by any chance?	**Nǐmen hái yǒu xiē shénme cài mèi shàng ma?** 你们还有些什么菜没上吗？
I'm on a salt-free diet	**Wǒ bù chī yán** 我不吃盐
I can't eat pork	**Wǒ bù néng chī zhūròu** 我不能吃猪肉

您/你们要什么？
Nín/nǐmen yào shénme?

What would you like?

要点菜了吗？
Yàodiǎn càile ma?

Have you decided?

要不要先来杯饮料？
Yàobuyào xiān lái bēi yǐnliào?

Would you like a drink first?

喝点什么？
Hē diǎn shénme?

What would you like to drink?

我们刚卖完…
Wǒmen gāng mài wán...

We've run out of...

菜来了，请用吧
Cài láile, qǐng yòng ba

Enjoy your meal

饭菜做得怎么样？
Fàncài zuò de zěnmeyàng?

Is everything all right?

我可以收盘子了吗？
Wǒ kěyǐ shōupánzi le ma?

May I clear the table?

I can't have sugar	**Wǒ bù néng chī táng** 我不能吃糖
I'm on a fat-free diet	**Wǒ bù chī yóunì de shíwù** 我不吃油腻的食物
I can't have spicy food	**Wǒ bù néng chī là de dōngxi** 我不能吃辣的东西
We'll have what those people are having	**Wǒmen yào tāmen chī de nàzhǒng** 我们要他们吃的那种
I'd like...	**Yào yí ge... /Lái yí ge...** 要一个… / 来一个…
We're not having Beijing Duck	**Wǒmen bù chī Běijīng Kǎoyā** 我们不吃北京烤鸭
Could I have some more rice, please?	**Zài gěi wǒ lái diǎnr mǐfàn** 再给我来点儿米饭
Could I have another bottle of boiled water/ wine, please?	**Zài gěi wǒ yì píng liángkāishuǐ/jiǔ** 再给我一瓶凉开水 / 酒
Could I have another portion of..., please?	**Qǐng zài gěi wǒ yí fèn....** 请再给我一份…
Could I have the salt and pepper, please?	**Qǐng gěi wǒ yán hé hújiāo** 请给我盐和胡椒
Could I have a napkin, please?	**Qǐng gěi wǒ yí zhāng cānján** 请给我一张餐巾
Could I have a teaspoon, please?	**Qǐng gěi wǒ yí ge cháchí** 请给我一个茶匙
Could I have an ashtray, please?	**Qǐng gěi wǒ yí ge yānhuīgāng** 请给我一个烟灰缸
Could I have some matches, please?	**Qǐng gěi wǒ yí hé huǒchái** 请给我一盒火柴
Could I have some toothpicks, please	**Qǐng gěi wǒ jǐ gēn yáqiān** 请给我几根牙签
Could I have a glass of boiled water, please?	**Qǐng gěi wǒ yí bēi liángkāishuǐ** 请给我一杯凉开水

Could I have a straw please?	**Qǐng gěi wǒ yí gēn xīguǎn** 请给我一根吸管
Enjoy your meal	**Cài qí le, nín/nǐmen qǐng ba!** 菜齐了，您／你们请吧！
You eat as well!	**Nǐ yě chība!** 你也吃吧！
Cheers!	**Gānbēi!** 干杯！
The next round's on me	**Xiàcì wǒ qǐngkè** 下次我请客
Could we have a doggy bag, please?	**Qǐng gěi wǒmen dǎbāo** 请给我们打包

4.3 The bill

See also 8.2 Settling the bill

How much is this dish?	**Zhè pán cài duōshao qián?** 这盘菜多少钱？
Could I have the bill, please?	**Qǐng gěi wǒ zhàngdān** 请给我账单
All together	**Yígòng....** 一共…
Everyone pays separately	**Wǒmen gè fù gè de zhàngdān ba** 我们各付各的账单吧
Let's go Dutch	**Zámen píngtān zhàngdān ba!** 咱们平摊账单吧
Could we have the menu again, please?	**Qǐng zài gěi wǒmen càidān kànkan** 请再给我们菜单看看
The...is not on the bill	**Zhàngdān shàng méiyǒu zhè ge...** 账单上没有这个…

4.4 Complaints

It's taking a very long time	**Wǒ yǐjīng děngle hěn jiǔ le** 我已经等了很久了
This must be a mistake	**Wǒ kàn nǐmen gǎocuò le** 我看你们搞错了
This is not what I ordered	**Zhè bú shì wǒ diǎn de cài** 这不是我点的菜
I ordered...	**Wǒ yào de shì...** 我要的是…
There's a dish missing	**Hái chà yí ge cài** 还差一个菜
The plate is broken/ not clean	**Zhè ge (pán) quēkǒule/bù gānjìng** 这个(盘)缺口了／不干净
The food's cold	**Zhè pán cài lěngle** 这盘菜冷了
The food's not fresh	**Zhè pán cài bù xīnxiān** 这盘菜不新鲜
The food's too salty/ sweet/spicy	**Zhè pán cài tài xián/tián/là le** 这盘菜太咸/甜／辣了
The food is off/has gone bad	**Zhè pán cài sōu/huài le** 这盘菜馊／坏了
Could I have something else instead of this?	**Qǐng gěi wǒ huàn yí ge biéde cài** 请给我换一个别的菜
The bill/this amount is not right	**Zhàngdān suànde bú duì** 账单算得不对
We didn't have this	**Wǒmen méiyǒu yào zhè ge cài** 我们没有要这个菜
There's no toilet paper in the restroom	**Xǐshǒujiān lǐ méiyǒu shǒuzhǐ/ wèishēngzhǐ le** 洗手间没有手纸／卫生纸了
Will you call the manager, please?	**Qǐng jiào nǐmen de jīnglǐ lái** 请叫你们的经理来

4.5 Paying a compliment

That was a sumptuous meal	**Fàncài hěn fēngshèng** 饭菜很丰盛
The food was excellent	**Fàncài hǎojíle** 饭菜好极了
The...in particular was delicious	**Tèbié shì..., tài hǎochī le** 特别…, 太好吃了

4.6 Requests

Please give me...	**Qǐng gěi wǒ...** 请给我…
the menu	**càidān** 菜单
a pair of chopsticks	**yí shuāng kuàizi** 一双筷子
a fork	**yí bǎ cānchā/chāzi** 一把餐叉 / 叉子
a knife	**yí bǎ dāozi** 一把刀子
a plate	**yí ge pánzi** 一个盘子
a bowl	**yí ge wǎn** 一个碗
a spoon	**yì bǎ tāngchí** 一把汤匙
a ladle	**yì bǎ sháozi/tāngsháo** 一把勺子 / 汤勺
salt	**yán** 盐
pepper	**hújiāo** 胡椒
sugar	**táng** 糖
fruit	**shuǐguǒ** 水果
ice cream	**bīngjīlíng/bīngqílín** 冰激凌/冰淇淋
meat	**ròu (shí)** 肉(食)
salad	**shālā** 沙拉
main course	**zhǔcài** 主菜
side dishes/vegetables	**pèicài/shūcài** 配菜/蔬菜
service charge (included)	**fíwùfèi (yǐ bāokuò zài nèi)** 服务费(已包括在内)

soup	**tāng** 汤
specialities	**tèsècài** 特色菜
snacks	**xiāochī** 小吃
bread	**miànbāo** 面包
cakes/desserts	**dàn gāo/tiánshí** 蛋糕/甜食
noodles	**miàntiáo** 面条
vegetables	**shūcài** 蔬菜
fish	**yú** 鱼

4.7 Drinks

hot/cold cocoa	**rè/lěng kěkě** 热/冷可可
hot/cold milk	**rè/lěng niúnǎi** 热/冷牛奶
black tea	**hóngchá (bù jiā nǎi)** 红茶(不加奶)
English tea (with milk)	**nǎichá** 奶茶
coffee	**kāfēi** 咖啡
jasmine tea	**mòlì huāchá** 茉莉花茶
beer	**píjiǔ** 啤酒
orange juice	**júzizhī/liǔdīngzhī** 桔子汁/柳丁汁
mineral water	**kuàng quánshuǐ** 矿泉水
soda water	**sūdǎshuǐ** 苏打水
coca cola	**kěkǒu kělè** 可口可乐
brandy	**báilándǐ** 白兰地
whisky	**wéishìjì** 威士忌
champagne	**xiāngbīnjiǔ** 香槟酒
red wine	**hóng pútaojiǔ/hóngjiǔ** 红葡萄酒/红酒
white wine	**bái pútaojiǔ/báijiǔ** 白葡萄酒/白酒

4.8 The menu

Chinese dishes	**Zhōngcān** 中餐
assorted cold dishes	**lěng pīnpán/liángcài** 冷拼盘／凉菜
pickled cabbage	**pàocài** 泡菜
sautéd chicken with hot pepper and peanuts	**Jiàngbào jīdīng** 酱爆鸡丁
fish with sweet and sour sauce	**Tángcù yú** 糖醋鱼
sautéd fried prawns	**Zhá-pēng xiāduàn** 炸烹虾段
sweet and sour pork	**Gǔlǎoròu** 咕唠肉
sautéd mutton slice with scallion	**Cōngbào yángròu** 葱爆羊肉
sautéd beef with onion	**Yángcōng chǎo niúròu** 洋葱炒牛肉
sautéd fresh mushroom and choi sam	**Xiānggū càixīn** 香菇菜心
sautéd bean-curd with brown sauce	**Hóngshāo dòufu** 红烧豆腐
steamed rice	**mǐfàn** 米饭
fried rice with eggs	**jidàn chǎofàn** 鸡蛋炒饭
Western dishes	**Xīcān** 西餐
soft boiled egg	**zhǔ jīdān** 煮鸡蛋
scrambled egg	**chǎo jīdān** 炒鸡蛋
toast	**kǎo miànbāo piàn/tǔsī** 烤面包片／吐司
sandwich	**sānmíngzhì** 三明治
butter	**huángyóu/nǎiyóu** 黄油／奶油
cheese	**nǎilào/rǔlào** 奶酪／乳酪
jam	**guǒjiàng** 果酱
pizza	**bǐsābǐng** 比萨饼

5 Getting Around

5.1	**Asking directions**	**72**
5.2	**Traffic signs**	**74**
5.3	**The car**	**75**
	The parts of a car	*76-77*
5.4	**The gas station**	**75**
5.5	**Breakdowns and repairs**	**78**
5.6	**Bicycles/mopeds**	**80**
	The parts of a bicycle	*82-83*
5.7	**Renting a vehicle**	**81**
5.8	**Getting a lift**	**84**

5. Getting Around

5.1 Asking directions

Excuse me, could I ask you something?
Láojià, wǒ kěyǐ wèn nín yíxià ma?
劳驾，我可以问您一下吗？

I've lost my way
Wǒ mílù le
我迷路了

Is there a ... around here?
Fùjìn yǒu méiyǒu...?
附近有没有…？

Excuse me, what direction is ...?
Qǐngwèn, ...zài nǎ ge fāngxiàng?
请问，…在哪个方向？

Excuse me, am I going in the right direction for ...?
Qǐngwèn, ...zǒu zhè ge fāngxiàng duì ma?
请问，…走这个方向对吗？

bus stop
qìchēzhàn
汽车站

railway station
huǒchēzhàn
火车站

Could you tell me how to get to...?
Qǐngwèn, ...zěnme zǒu?
请问，…怎么走？

How many kilometers Is it to...?
Dào...yǒu duōshao gōnglǐ?
到…有多少公里？

Is it far?
Yuǎn bu yuǎn?
远不远？

Can I walk there?
Kěyǐ zǒulù qù ma?
可以走路去吗？

Is it difficult to find?
Hǎo bu hǎo zhǎo?
好不好找？

我不请楚, 我不认识这里的路
Wǒ bù qǐngchu, wǒ bú rènshi zhèlǐ de lù

I don't know, I don't know my way around here

你走错了
Nǐ zǒu cuòle

You're going the wrong way

你要往回走
Nǐ yào wǎng huí zǒu

You have to go back

从那儿开始, 跟着路牌走
Cóng nàr kāishǐ, gēnzhe lùpái zǒu

From there on just follow the signs

到那边再问
Dào nàbiān zài wèn

When you get there, ask again

一直走下去
Yīzhí zǒu xiàqù

Go straight ahead

过
Guò

Cross

转右 / 转左
Zhuǎnyòu/Zhuǎnzuǒ

Turn right/Turn left

顺着 / 沿着
shùnzhe/yánzhe

Follow

路 / 街
lù/jiē
road/street

高架桥
gāojiàqiáo
overpass

楼房
lóufáng
the building

河
hé
river

隧道
suìdào
tunnel

街角 / 拐角 (角落)
jiējiǎo/guǎijiǎo (jiǎoluò)
at the corner

红绿灯 / 交通灯
hónglǜdēng/jiāotōngdēng
traffic light

桥
qiáo
bridge

箭头标志
jiàntóu biāozhì
arrow sign

5.2 Traffic signs

交通标志
jiāotōng biāozhì
traffic signs

十字路口
shízìlùkǒu
intersection/
crossroads

汽车故障服务处
**qìchē gùzhàng
fúwùchù**
road assistance
(breakdown
service)

停(车)
tíng (chē)
stop (vehicle)

限时停车
xiànshí tíngchē
parking for a
limited period

加油站
jiāyóuzhàn
service station

不准堵塞
bùzhǔn dǔsè
do not obstruct

路面损坏 / 不平
**lùmiàn sǔnhuài/
bùpíng**
broken/uneven
surface

当心
dāngxīn
beware

需用雪链
xūyòng xuěliàn
snow chains
required

前面路窄
qiánmiàn lùzhǎi
narrowing in the road

交通道 / 人行道
jiāotōngdào/rénxíngdào
traffic island/pedestrian walk

进隧道请开前灯
jìn suìdào qǐng kāi qiándēng
turn on headlights (in the
tunnel)

收费停车 / 专用车位
**shōufèi tíngchē/zhuānyòng
chēwèi**
paying carpark/
parking reserved for

靠右行 / 靠左行
kào yòu xíng/kào zuǒ xíng
keep right/left

当心山上石头
dāngxīn shānshàng shítou
beware of falling rocks

监控车库 / 停车场
jiānkòng chēkù/tíngchēchǎng
supervised garage/parking lot

(必须显示)停放车标
(bìxū xiǎnshì) tíngfàng chē biāo
parking disk (compulsory)

(铁路公路)交叉口
(tiělù gōnglù) jiāochākǒu
grade crossing

下一段路多雨或雪
xià yíduàn lù duōyǔ huò xuě
rain or ice for...kms

停车被拖走地带
tíngchē bèi tuōzǒu dìdài
tow-away area (both sides of
the road)

绕道
ràodào
detour

道路阻塞
dàolù zǔsè
road blocked

换行车道
**huànháng
chēdào**
change lanes

道路封闭
dàolù fēngbì
road closed

出口
chūkǒu
exit

紧急行车道
jǐnjí xíngchēdào
emergency lane

车道
chēdào
driveway

急转弯
jízhuǎnwān
curves

危险
wéixiǎn
danger(ous)

不准驶入
bùzhǔn shǐrù
no entry

慢行
mànxíng
slow down

圆盘地带
yuán pán dìdài
disk zone

前面修路
qiánmiàn xiūlù
roadworks ahead

先使用车道权
xiān shǐyòng chēdàoquán
right of way

不准超车
bù zhǔn chāochē
no passing

路不开放
lù bù kāifàng
road closed

不准搭乘他人便车
bù zhǔn dāchéng tārén biànchē
no hitchhiking

不准停车
bù zhǔn tíngchē
no parking

载重卡车
zàizhòng kǎchē
heavy trucks

不准转右／左
bù zhǔn zhuǎnyòu/zuǒ
no right/left turn

单行道
dānxíng dào
one way

净空高度
jìngkōng gāodù
maximum height

先使用车道权在路尾
xiān shǐyòng chēdàoquán
  zài lùwěi
right of way at end of road

隧道
suìdào
tunnel

最高速度
zuìgāo sùdù
maximum speed

通行费
tōngxíng fèi
toll payment

5.3 The car

See the diagram on page 77

● **The speed limits for vehicles** vary in different cities and on different roads. Generally speaking, the speed limit for cars is 110 km/h on non-urban highways, 80 km/h on main roads and 70 km/h on built-up areas. For motorcycles the limits are 60 km/h on main roads, 50 km/h on build-up areas. Motorcycles are not allowed to travel on highways.

5.4 The gas station

● **The cost of gas in China** for unleaded #93 is around 7.25 RMB/liter, unleaded #90 is 6.75 RMB/liter, and diesel is 7.15 RMB/liter. Leaded petrol and LPG are cheaper. Mopeds are generally used in non-urban areas. There are strict restrictions on their use in cities. Along with bicycles, they are limited to special lanes in urban roads.

How many kilometers to the next gas station, please?

Qǐng wèn, dào xià yí ge jiāyóuzhàn yǒu duō yuǎn?
请问，到下一个加油站有多远？

The parts of a car

(the diagram shows the numbered parts)

1	battery	电池	diànchí
2	rear light	后灯	hòudēng
3	rear-view mirror	后视镜	hòushìjìng
	backup light	后补灯	hòubǔdēng
4	aerial	天线	tiānxiàn
	car radio	收音机	shōuyīnjī
5	gas tank	油箱	yóuxiāng
6	spark plugs	火花塞	huǒhuāsài
	fuel pump	燃油泵	rányóubèng
7	side mirror	侧视镜	cèshìjìng
8	bumper	保险杆	bǎoxiǎn'gān
	carburettor	汽化器	qìhuàqì
	crankcase	曲柄轴箱	qūbǐng zhóuxiāng
	cylinder	汽缸	qìgāng
	ignition	点火装置	diǎnhuǒ zhuāngzhì
	warning light	警告灯	jǐnggàodēng
	generator	发电机	fādiànjī
	accelerator	油门	yóumén
	handbrake	手刹车	shǒushāchē
	valve	活门	huómén
9	muffler	消声器	xiāoshēngqì
10	trunk	车尾箱	chēwěixiāng
11	headlight	前灯	qiāndēng
	crank shaft	曲轴	qūzhóu
12	air filter	过滤器	guòlǜqì
	fog lamp	雾灯	wùdēng
13	engine block	发动机	fādòngjī
	camshaft	凸轮轴	tūlúnzhóu
	oil filter/pump	滤油器 / 滤油泵	lǜyóuqì/lǜyóubèng
	dipstick	量油尺	liángyóuchǐ
	pedal	脚刹车	jiǎoshāchē
14	door	车门	chēmén
15	radiator	水箱	shuǐxiāng
16	brake disc	刹车碟	shāchēdié
	spare wheel	备用轮胎	bèiyòng lúntāi
17	indicator	指示器	zhǐshìqì
18	windshield wiper	挡风玻璃雨刷	dǎngfēng bōli yǔshuā
19	shock absorbers	减震器	jiǎnzhènqì
	sunroof	遮阳蓬顶	zhēyáng péngdǐng
	spoiler	车尾装置	chēwěi zhuāngzhì

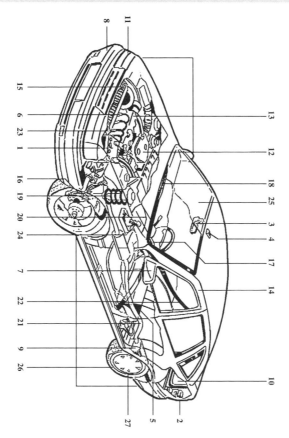

20	steering column	方向柱	fāngxiàngzhù
	steering wheel	方向盘	fāngxiàngpán
21	exhaust pipe	排气管	páiqìguǎn
22	seat belt	安全带	ānquándài
	fan	鼓风器	gǔfēngjī
23	distributor	分配器	fēnpèiqì
	cables	电线	diànxiàn
24	gear shift	变速箱	biànsùxiāng
25	windshield	挡风玻璃	dǎngfēng bōli
	water pump	水泵	shuǐbèng
26	wheel	车轮	chēlún
27	hubcap	轮盖	lúngài
	piston	活塞	huósài

I would like...liters of	**Wǒ yào....gōngshēng** 我要…公升
– unleaded #93	**jiǔshísānhào wúqiān qìyóu** 九十三号无铅汽油
– unleaded #90	**jiǔshíhào wúqiān qìyóu** 九十号无铅汽油
– leaded petrol	**hánqiān qìyóu** 含铅汽油
– LPG gas	**méiqì** 煤气
– diesel	**cháiyóu** 柴油
... dollars worth of gas	**...yuán de qìyóu** …元的汽油
Fill her up, please	**Qǐng jiāmǎn yóuxiāng** 请加满油箱
Could you check...	**Qǐng gěi wǒ jiǎnchá...** 请给我检查…
– the oil level	**jīyóu gòu bu gòu mǎn?** 机油够不够满?
– the tire pressure	**lúntāi qì gòu bu gòu?** 轮胎气够不够?
Could you change the oil, please?	**Qǐng gěi wǒ huàn jīyóu** 请给找换机油
Could you clean the windshield, please?	**Qǐng gěi wǒ cāyicā dǎngféng bōli** 请给我擦一擦挡风玻璃
Could you wash the car, please?	**Qǐng gěi wǒ cāyicā chē** 请给我擦一擦车

5.5 Breakdowns and repairs

My car has broken down, could you give me a hand?	**Wǒde chē huàile, nǐ néng bāngzhu wǒ ma?** 我的车坏了, 你能帮助我吗?

I have run out of gas	**Wǒde chē méiyǒu qìyóu le** 我的车没有汽油了
I've locked the keys in the car	**Wǒ bǎ yàoshi suǒ zài chē lǐmiàn le** 我把钥匙锁在车里面了
The car/motorbike won't start	**Wǒde qìchè/mótuōchē bù néng qǐdòng** 我的汽车 / 摩托车不能起动
Could you contact the breakdown service for me, please?	**Qǐng gěi wǒ liánluò gùzhàng fúwùchù** 请给我联络故障服务处
Could you call a garage for me, please?	**Qǐng gěi wǒ jiào xiūchēchǎng** 请给我叫修车厂
Could you give me a lift to...?	**Nǐ kě bu kěyǐ dài wǒ dào... ?** 你可不可以带我到…?
– the nearest garage?	**zuì jìn de xiūchēchǎng?** 最近的修车厂?
– the nearest town?	**zuì jìn de xiāngzhèn?** 最近的乡镇?
– the nearest telephone booth?	**zuì jìn de gōngyòng diànhuà?** 最近的公用电话?
– the nearest emergency phone?	**zuì jìn de jǐnjí diànhuà?** 最近的紧急电话?
Can we take my motorcycle?	**Nǐ kěyǐ yùn wǒde mótuōchē ma?** 你可以运我的摩托车吗?
Could you tow me to a garage?	**Kěyǐ tuō wǒde chē dào xiūchēchǎng ma?** 可以拖我的车到修车厂吗?
There's probably something wrong	**....kěnéng yǒu máobìng** …可能有毛病
Can you fix it?	**Kěyǐ xiūlǐ ma?** 可以修理吗?
Could you fix my tire?	**Kěyǐ bǔ lúntāi ma?** 可以补轮胎吗?
Could you change this wheel?	**Kěyǐ gěi wǒ huàn zhè ge lúntāi ma?** 可以给我换这个轮胎吗?

Can you fix it so it'll get me to...?	**Kěyǐ gěi wǒ xiūyixiū, ràng wǒ néng kāidào...** 可以给我修一修，让我能开到…
Which garage can help me?	**Nǎ yì jiā xiūchēchǎng néng bāngzhu wǒ?** 哪一家修车厂能帮助我？
When will my car/bicycle be ready?	**Wǒde qìchē/zìxíngchē shénme shíhou néng xiūhǎo?** 我的汽车／自行车什么时候能修好？
Have you already finished?	**Nǐ gěi wǒ xiūhǎo le méiyǒu?** 你给我修好了没有？
Can I wait for it here?	**Wǒ kěyǐ zài zhèr děng nǐ xiūhǎo ma?** 我可以在这儿等你修好吗？
How much will it cost?	**Xiūlǐfèi shì duōshao?** 修理费是多少？
Could you itemize the bill?	**Kěyǐ bǎ xiūlǐ de xiàngmù liè gěi wǒ kàn ma?** 可以把修理的项目列给我看吗？
Please give me a receipt for insurance purposes.	**Qǐng gěi wǒ kāi zhāng fāpiào, wǒ xūyào gěi bǎoxiǎn gōngsī kàn** 请给我开张发票，我需要给保险公司看

5.6 Bicycles/mopeds

See the diagram on page 83

● **The bicycle** is the main means of transport for ordinary citizens in China. There are tens of millions of bicycles in China and you will find that there is at least one bicycle for every family. Mopeds are mechanized bicycles for longer distance commuting and because of their speed, the wearing of crash helmets is compulsory. People rely on bicycles and mopeds to take them to work, do their shopping and for recreational purposes. As China modernizes, bicycles are increasingly barred from highways and ring-roads. In addition to bicycles, motorcycle riders are required to wear crash helmets.

我没有你要的配件
Wǒ méiyǒu nǐ yào de pèijiàn

I don't have parts for your vehicle

我要去别的地方给你找配件
**Wǒ yào qù bié dì dìfāng gěi nǐ
  zhǎo pèijiàn**

I have to get the parts from
  somewhere else

我需要给你订配件
Wǒ xūyào gěi nǐ dìng pèijiàn

I have to order the parts

那需要半天时间
Nà xūyào bàntiān shíjiān

That'll take half a day

那需要一天时间
Nà xūyào yītiān shíjiān

That'll take a day

那需要几天时间
Nà xūyào jǐtiān shíjiān

That'll take a few days

那需要一个星期时间
Nà xūyào yīgè xīngqí shíjiān

That'll take a week

修理费超过汽车／自行车的价值
**Xiūlǐ fèi chāoguò qìchē/zìxíngchē
  de jiàzhí**

Your car/bicycle is a write-off

你的汽车／摩托车／助动车／
自行车不能修
**Nǐ de qìchē/mótuōchē/zhùdòngchē/
  zìxíngchē bùnéng xiū**

It can't be repaired

你的汽车／摩托车／助动车／
自行车…点就能修好
**Nǐ de qìchē/mótuōchē/zhùdòngchē/
  zìxíngchē …diǎn jiù néng xiūhǎo**

The car/motor bike/moped/
bicycle will be ready at...o'clock

5.7 Renting a vehicle

I'd like to rent a...

Wǒ xiǎng zū yí liàng...
我想租一辆…

Do I need a (special)
  license for that?

Wǒ xūyào (tèbiéde) zhízhào ma?
我需要（特别的）执照吗？

I'd like to rent the...for...

Wǒ xiǎng zū...
我想租…

– a day

yì tiān
一天

The parts of a bicycle

(the diagram shows the numbered parts)

1	rear light	后灯	hòudēng
2	rear wheel	后轮	hòulún
3	(luggage) carrier	车筐	chē kuāng
4	fork	轮叉	lúnchā
5	bell	车铃	chēlíng
	inner tube	轮胎内胎	lúntāi nèitāi
	tire	轮胎	lúntāi
6	peddle crank	脚踏曲柄	jiǎotà qūbǐng
7	gear change	变速器	biànsùqì
	wire	金属线	jīnshǔxiàn
	generator	发动器	fādòngqì
	bicycle trailer	拖载自行车的拖车	tuōzài zìxíngchē de tuōchē
	frame	车架	chējià
8	wheel guard	护车轮装置	hù chēlún zhuāngzhì
9	chain	链带	liàndài
	chain guard	护链带装置	hù liàndài zhuāngzhì
	odometer	里程表	lǐchéngbiǎo
	child's seat	小孩座	xiǎoháizuò
10	headlight	前灯	qiándēng
11	pedal	踏脚板	tàjiǎobǎn
12	pump	打气筒	dǎqìtǒng
13	reflector	反射镜	fǎnshèjìng
14	brake shoe	刹车片	shāchēpiàn
15	brake cable	刹车线	shāchēxiàn
16	anti theft device	防盗装置	fángdào zhuāngzhì
17	carrier straps	运载布带	yùnzài bùdài
	tachometer	速度计	sùdùjì
18	spoke	钢丝	gāngsī
19	mudguard	挡泥板	dǎngníbǎn
20	handlebar	把手	bǎshǒu
21	chain wheel	链轮	liànlún
	toe clip	踏板扣	tàbǎnkòu
22	crank axle	曲柄轴	qūbǐngzhóu
	drum brake	鼓刹车	gǔ shāchē
23	rim	钢圈	gāngquān
24	valve	活门	huómén
25	gear cable	变速线	biànsùxiàn

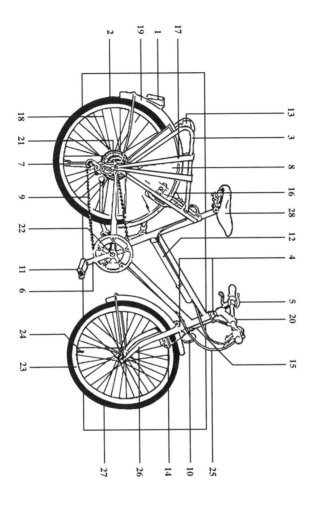

26	fork	轮叉	**lúnchā**
27	front wheel	前轮	**qiánlún**
28	seat	座位	**zuòwèi**

– two days	**liǎng tiān** 两天
How much is that per day/week?	**Zūjīn yì tiān/xīngqī duōshao qián?** 租金一天／星期多少钱？
How much is the deposit?	**Yājīn yào fù duōshao qián?** 押金要付多少钱？
Could I have a receipt for the deposit?	**Qǐng gěi wǒ yājīn shōujù** 请给我押金收据
Does that include insurance?	**Shōufèi bāokuò bǎoxiǎnfèi ma?** 收费包括保险费吗？
What time can I pick the...up?	**Wǒ shénme shíhou lái qǔ chē?** 我什么时候来取车？
When does the...have to be back?	**Chē shénme shíhou yào huán?** 车什么时候要还？

5.8 Getting a lift

Where are you heading?	**Nǐ yào qù nǎr?** 你要去哪儿？
Can you give me a lift?	**Wǒ kěyǐ dā nǐde chē qù ma?** 我可以搭你的车去吗？
Can my friend come too?	**Wǒde péngyou yě néng lái ma?** 我的朋友也能来吗？
I'd like to go to...	**Wǒ xiǎng qù...** 我想去…
Is that on the way to...?	**Zhè shìbushì qù...de lù?** 这是不是去…的路？
Could you drop me off...?	**Nǐ kěyǐ zài...ràng wǒ xiàchē ma?** 你可以在…让我下车吗？
Could you drop me off here?	**Nǐ kěyǐ zài zhèlǐ ràng wǒ xiàchē ma?** 你可以在这里让我下车吗？
– at the entrance to the highway?	**zài gōnglù de jìnkǒu** 在公路的进口

– in the center?	**zài gōnglù zhōngjiān** 在公路中间
– at the next intersection?	**zài xià yí ge shízìlùkǒu** 在下一个十字路口
Could you stop here, please?	**Nǐ kěyǐ zài zhèlǐ tíngchē ma?** 你可以在这里停车吗？
I'd like to get out here	**Wǒ xiǎng zài zhèlǐ xiàchē** 我想在这里下车
Thanks for the lift	**Fēicháng gǎnxiè gěi wǒ dāchē!** 非常感谢给我搭车！

6 Arrival and Departure

6.1	General	87
6.2	Customs	88
6.3	Luggage	90
6.4	Tickets	91
6.5	Information	92
6.6	Airports	94
6.7	Subway trains	96
6.8	Long-distance trains	98
6.9	Buses	100
6.10	Taxis	101

6. Arrival and Departure

6.1 General

● **For most cities in China**, ordinary people mainly commute by bus (**gōnggòngqìchē** 公共汽车) with the result that buses are often very congested for most hours of the day and night. Although services are frequent, bus stops are often quite a distance apart so there are just too many people waiting to get on at each stop. Foreigners are sometimes amazed by the number of people that can be packed into a bus. For those prepared to take up the challenge of getting into one, make sure that you have exact money for the ride as they don't give change. (Fares can be as low as a few cents to a dollar or two.) Increasingly in large cities, some routes are now serviced by more luxurious buses often labelled as air-conditioned buses. They are more comfortable and the fare is about twice as much as for the ordinary buses.

Most cities now have taxis and mini-vans to provide faster commuter services. The latter means of transport is increasingly preferred by ordinary commuters as they are less expensive than taxis and passengers can nominate where to stop. There are two types of taxis: the less expensive type carrying up to 3 passengers, and a larger, more comfortable 5-seater which costs more to hire. In addition to cash payment, some of these taxis also offer a credit card system for payment.

Only Beijing, Shanghai and Guangzhou have subways (**dìtiě** 地铁). Tickets are purchased at the stations. Since 2007 the introduction of high-speed rail in China (**Zhōngguó gāosù tiělù** 中国高速铁路) has enabled commuters to travel across states speedily in trains that have an average speed of 200 km/h. The Shanghai Maglev train, for example, is able to go beyond 380 km/h but averages 250 km/h because of track constraints. Using such high-speed trains enables the commuter to cut down substantially his/her traveling time.

Inter-city travel is mostly done by trains and planes although boats are used to transport passengers along the considerable number of waterways in China. Long-distance travel is mostly done on trains, although domestic air travel has become popular among middle-income earners as airfares are now affordable.

6.2 Customs

● **In China**, you should always carry with you a valid passport. Strictly speaking, visitors planning to stay at the same address for more than one week need permission from the Police Department. This only becomes a necessity if you plan to study, work or live in China. To drive a car or motorbike, you need to do a test to obtain a valid Chinese driving licence.

Import and export specifications:

Foreign currency: you need to declare amounts of foreign currency greater that US$5,000 or the equivalent, or RMB 20,000, brought into China.

Alcohol: 1.5 liter spirits or liquor, 1.5 liter wine
Tobacco: 400 cigarettes, 100 cigars, 500g tobacco

You must be aged 17 to import alcohol and tobacco and 15 to import coffee and tea. The above restrictions apply to all alcohol and tobacco purchased in duty-free shops.

请填一下入境卡
Qǐng tián yíxià rùjìng kǎ

Please fill in the arrival card

请出示你的护照
Qǐng chūshì nǐde hùzhào

Your passport, please

请给我看看你的签证
Qǐng gěi wǒ kànkàn nǐde qiānzhèng

Your visa, please

你去哪个城市?
Nǐ qù nǎge chéngshì?

Where are you going?

你(们)要在这里住多少天?
Nǐ (men) yào zài zhèlǐ zhù duōshao tiān?

How long are you planning to stay?

你(们)有没有什么要申报？
Nǐ (men) yǒu méiyǒu shénme yào shēnbào?

Do you have anything to declare?

请打开这个箱子
Qǐng dǎkāi zhè ge xiāngzi

Open this suitcase, please

My children are entered on this passport	**Wǒ háizi de míngzi zài wǒde hùzhào shàng** 我孩子的名字在我的护照上
I'm traveling through	**Wǒ zhǐ shì jīngguò zhèr** 我只是经过这儿
I'm going on vacation to...	**Wǒ yào dào...dùjià** 我要到⋯度假
I'm on a business trip	**Wǒ shì lái chūchāi de** 我是来出差的
I don't know how long I'll be staying	**Wǒ hái bù zhīdao yào zài zhèlǐ zhù duō jiǔ** 我还不知道要在这里住多久
I'll be staying here for just a weekend	**Wǒ zài zhèlǐ zhǐ zhù yí ge zhōumò** 我在这里只住一个周末
I'll be staying here for a few days	**Wǒ zài zhèlǐ zhù jǐ tiān** 我在这里住几天
I'll be staying here a week	**Wǒ zài zhèlǐ zhù yí ge xīngqī** 我在这里住一个星期
I'll be staying here for two weeks	**Wǒ zài zhèlǐ zhù liǎng ge xīngqī** 我在这里住两个星期
I've got nothing to declare	**Wǒ méiyǒu shénme yào shēnbào de** 我没有什么要申报的
I have...	**Wǒ yǒu...** 我有⋯
a carton of cigarettes	**yì hé xiāngyān** 一盒香烟
a bottle of...	**yì píng...** 一瓶⋯

some souvenirs	**yìxiē jìniànpǐn** 一些纪念品
These are personal items	**Zhèxiē dōu shì wǒ zìjǐ yòng de dōngxi** 这些都是我自己用的东西
These are not new	**Zhèxiē dōu bú shì xīn de** 这些都不是新的
Here's the receipt	**Zhè shì shōujù** 这是收据
This is for private use	**Zhè shì wǒ sīrén yòng de** 这是我私人用的
How much import duty do I have to pay?	**Wǒ yào jiāo duōshao shuì?** 我要交多少税？
May I go now?	**Wǒ kěyǐ zǒu le ma?** 我可以走了吗？
Where do I pick up my lugguage?	**Dào nǎli qǔ xíngli?** 到哪里取行李？

6.3 Luggage

Porter!	**Fúwùyuán!** 服务员！
Could you take this luggage to...?	**Qǐng bāng wǒ bǎ zhè jiàn xíngli ná dào,,,** 请帮我把这件行李拿到…
How much do I owe you?	**Wǒ yào fù nǐ duōshao xiǎofèi?** 我要付你多少小费？
Where can I find a trolley?	**Wǒ zài nǎli néng zhǎodào xiǎo tuīchē?** 我在哪里能找到小推车？
Could you store this luggage for me?	**Qǐng gěi wǒ cúnxià zhè jiàn xíngli** 请给我存下这件行李
Where are the luggage lockers?	**Xíngli guìzi zài nǎli?** 行李柜子在哪里？
I can't get the locker open	**Wǒ dǎbukāi zhè ge guìzi** 我打不开这个柜子

How much is it per item per day?	**Cún yí jiàn xíngli yì tiān duōshao qián?** 存一件行李一天多少钱？
This is not my bag/suitcase	**Zhè bú shì wǒde lǚxíngbāo/xiāngzi** 这不是我的旅行包／箱子
My suitcase is damaged	**Wǒde xiāngzi bèi záhuàile** 我的箱子被砸坏了
There's one item/bag/suitcase missing	**Wǒ diūshīle yí jiàn xíngli/yí ge lǚxíngbāo/yí ge xiāngzi** 我丢失了一件行李／一个旅行包／一个箱子

 ## 6.4 Tickets

Where can I...?	**Wǒ shàng nǎr kěyǐ...** 我上哪儿可以…
– buy a ticket?	**mǎi piào?** 买票？
– reserve a seat?	**yùdìng wèizi?** 预订位子？
– reserve a flight?	**yùdìng jīpiào?** 预订机票？
Could I have...for...please?	**Wǒ néng bu néng mǎi...zhāng qù...de piào?** 我能不能买…张去…的票？
A one-way ticket to...please	**Qǐng gěi wǒ yì zhāng qù...de dānchéngpiào** 请给我一张去…的单程票
A return ticket to..., please	**Qǐng gěi wǒ yì zhāng qù...de láihuípiào** 请给我一张去…的来回票
I'd like to reserve a hard berth/soft berth	**Wǒ xiǎng yùdìng yì zhāng yìngwò/ruǎnwò** 我想预订一张硬卧／软卧

Arrival and Departure

6

I'd like to reserve a top/ middle/bottom berth in the hard berth car	**Wǒ xiǎng yùdìng yìngwò chēxiāng de shàngpù/zhōngpù/xiàpù** 我想预订硬卧车厢的上铺／中铺／下铺
I'd like to reserve a top/ bottom berth in the soft berth car	**Wǒ xiǎng yùdìng ruǎnwò chēxiāng shàngpù/xiàpù** 我想预订软卧车厢的上铺／下铺

6.5 Information

Where can I find a schedule?	**Nǎli yǒu shíkèbiǎo?** 哪里有时刻表？
Where's the info desk?	**Fúwùtái zài nǎli?** 服务台在哪里？
Do you have a city map with the bus/subway routes on it?	**Yǒu méiyǒu shìqū gōnggòngqìchē/ dìtiě de lùxiàntú?** 有没有市区公共汽车／地铁的路线图？
Do you have a schedule?	**Yǒu méiyǒu shíkèbiǎo?** 有没有时刻表？
Will I get my deposit back?	**Néng bu néng náhuí yājīn?** 能不能拿回押金？
I'd like to confirm/cancel/ change my reservation for/my trip to...	**Wǒ xiǎng quèrèn/qǔxiāo/gǎibiàn wǒ yùdìng qù...de lǚchéng** 我想确认／取消／改变我预订去…的旅程
I'd like to go to...	**Wǒ xiǎng qù...** 我想去…
What is the quickest way to get there?	**Qù...zuìkuài de lùchéng shì nǎ yì tiáo?** 去…最快的路程是哪一条？
How much is a single/ return to...?	**Qù...de dānchéng/láihuípiào shì duōshao qián?** 去…的单程／来回票是多少钱？
Do I have to pay extra?	**Yào duō fùqián ma?** 要多付钱吗？

How much luggage am I allowed?	**Kěyǐ xiédài duōshao xíngli?** 可以携带多少行李？
Do I have to change (buses/trains)/flights?	**Yào zhuǎn chē (qìchē/huǒchē)/fēijī ma?** 要转车(汽车／火车)／飞机吗？
Where do I change (buses/trains)/flights?	**Zài nǎli zhuǎn chē (qìchē/huǒchē)/fēijī?** 在哪里转车(汽车／火车)／飞机？
Will there be any stopovers?	**Zhōngtú yào tíngliú ma?** 中途要停留吗？
Does the boat stop at any other ports on the way?	**Kèchuán tú zhōng yào tíng qítā mǎtóu ma?** 客船途中要停其他码头吗？
Does the train/bus stop at...?	**Huǒchē/qìchē zài...tíng ma?** 火车／汽车在…停吗？
Where do I get off?	**Zài nǎli xià (chē/chuán)?** 在哪里下(车／船)？
Is there a connection to...?	**Qù...yǒu liányùn ma?** 去…有连运吗？
How long do I have to wait?	**Yào děng duō jiǔ?** 要等多久？
When does the bus/train leave?	**Zhè bān qìchē/lièchē shénme shíhou kāichē?** 这班汽车／列车什么时候开车？
When does the boat leave?	**Zhè bān kèchuán shénme shíhou kāichuán?** 这班客船什么时候开船？
When does the plane leave?	**Zhè bān fēijī shénme shíhou qǐfēi?** 这班飞机什么时候起飞？
What time does the first/last (bus/train) leave?	**Tóubānchē/mòbānchē jǐ diǎn kāi?** 头班车／末班车几点开？
What time does the first/last boat leave?	**Tóubānchuán/mòbānchuán jǐ diǎn kāi?** 头班船／末班船几点开？
What time does the first/last plane leave?	**Tóubānjī/mòbānjī jǐ diǎn qǐfēi?** 头班机／末班机几点起飞？

What time does the next bus/train leave?	**Xià yì bān qìchē/lièchē jǐ diǎn kāi?** 下一班汽车／列车几点开？
What time does the next boat leave?	**Xià yì bān kèchuán jǐ diǎn kāi?** 下一班客船几点开？
What time does the next plane leave?	**Xià yì bān fēijī jǐ diǎn qǐfēi?** 下一班飞机几点起飞？
How long does...take?	**...xūyào duō cháng shíjiān?** …需要多长时间？
What time does...arrive in...?	**...shénme shíhou dào... ?** …什么时候到…？
Where does the bus/train to...leave from?	**Qù...de qìchē/lièchē jǐ diǎn kāichē?** 去…的汽车／列车几点开车？
Where does the boat to...leave from?	**Qù...de kèchuán jǐ diǎn kāichuán?** 去…的客船几点开船？
Where does the plane to...leave from?	**Qù...de fēijī jǐ diǎn qǐfēi?** 去…的飞机几点起飞？
Is this the train/bus to...?	**Zhè tàng lièchē/qìché qù...ma?** 这趟列车／汽车去…吗？

6.6 Airports

● **China's international airports** are located in large cities and provide high quality transportation. As in other international airport, make sure you have your passport and visa ready before you reach customs. And make sure you complete your arrival forms. Chinese customs are usually very helpful and friendly, but do not become angry or aggressive with them. This will only cause you a lot of trouble. Do ask for assistance if you have any doubt. And before you enter customs, make sure you complete the declaration form because there might be some particular items that need to be declared. The major international airports in China are:

Beijing Capital International Airport 北京首都国际机场,
Guangzhou Baiyun International Airport 广州白云国际机场,

Shanghai Hongqiao International Airport 上海虹桥国际机场,
Shenzhen Bao'an International Airport 深圳保安国际机场,
Shanghai Pudong International Airport 上海浦东国际机场,
Chengdu Shuangliu International Airport 成都双流国际机场,
Hainan Meilan International Airport 海南美兰国际机场,
Xiamen Gaoqi International Airport 厦门高崎国际机场,
Dalian Internaional Airport 大连国际机场, and
Kumming International Airport 昆明国际机场.

办理登机
bànlǐ dēngjī
check in

登机柜台
dēngjī guìtái
check-in counter

超重
chāozhòng
overweight

磅秤
bàngchèng
(weighing) scale

旅客
lǚkè
passenger

托运行李
tuōyùn xínglǐ
check-in luggage/bags

海关申请单
hǎiguān shēnqǐngdān
customs-declaration form

机票
jīpiào
ticket

登机证
dēngjīzhèng
boarding pass

护照
hùzhào
passport

签证
qiānzhèng
visa

表格
biǎogé
form

登机门
dēngjīmén
boarding gate

入境
rùjìng
immigration/arrival

机场安检
jīchǎng ānjiǎn
airport security

金属探测门
jīnshǔ tàncè mén
metal detector

航站
hángzhàn
terminal

免税店
miǎnshuìdiàn
duty-free store

接驳车
jiēbóchē
shuttle bus

出境
chūjìng
departure

走道
zǒudào
aisle

经济舱
jīngjìcāng
economy class

头等舱
tóuděngcāng
first class

座位
zòuwèi
seat

靠窗
kàochuāng
window

安全带
ānquándài
seat belt

I would like to check
in now

Wǒ yào bànlǐ dēngjī
我要办理登机

Where is…?	**Qǐngwèn, …zài nǎr?**
	请问, … 在哪？
– the check-in counter	**dēngjī guìtái**
	登机柜台
– the duty-free store	**miǎnshuì shāngdiàn**
	免税商店
May I see your ticket and passport?	**Wǒ kéyǐ kàn yíxià nínde jīpiào hé hùzhào ma?**
	我可以看一下您的机票和护照吗？
How many bags are you checking in?	**Nǐde tuōyùn xínglǐ yǒu jǐjiàn?**
	你的托运行李有几件？
I want a window and an aisle seat	**Wǒ yào yíge kàochuāng hé yíge zǒudào zuòwèi**
	我要一个靠窗和一个靠走道座位
Please put all metal objects in this tray and then walk through the metal detector	**Qǐng bǎ jīnshǔ wùpǐn fàng zài pánzi shàng, jiēzhe zǒuguò jīnshǔ tàncè mén**
	请把金属物品放在盘子上, 接着走过金属探测门
All passengers on flight DL 148 should proceed to gate eight for boarding	**DL 148 de lǚkè qǐng dào bāhào dēngjīmén dēngjī**
	DL 148的旅客请到八号登机门登机
Please fasten your seat belt	**Qǐng jìshàng ānquándài**
	请系上安全带
Please fill in the customs-declaration form	**Qǐng tiánxiě hǎiguān shēnqǐngbiǎo**
	请填写海关申请表
Are there any duty-free store at Terminal One?	**Qǐngwèn, dìyī hángzhàn yǒu miǎnshuì shāngdiàn ma?**
	请问, 第一航站有免税商店吗？

6.7 Subway trains

Your attention please, the next station is Qianmen	**Gèwèi chéngkè, nín hǎo! Lièchē yùnxíng qiánfāng shì Qiánménzhàn**
	各位乘客, 您好！列车运行前方是前门站

Passengers getting off at Qianmen, please get ready	**Zài Qiánménzhàn xiàchē de chéngkè, qǐng nín tíqián zuòhǎo zhǔnbèi** 在前门站下车的乘客, 请您提前作好准备
Qianmen station is a crowded station, please get ready beforehand and alight in an orderly manner	**Qiánménzhàn shàngxiàchē de chéngkè bǐjiào duō, qǐng nín tíqián zuòhǎo zhǔnbèi, àn shùnxù xiàchē** 前门站上下车的乘客比较多, 请您提前作好准备, 按顺序下车
Passengers changing for Gongzhufen Number 1 Line trains please get off at Fuxingmen	**Qiánwǎng Gōngzhǔfén fāngxiàng de chéngkè, qǐng zài Fùxīngmén xiàchē, huànchéng Yīxiàn lièchē** 前往公主坟方向的乘客, 请在复兴门下车, 换乘一线列车
The train to...is now arriving at platform...	**Kāiwǎng...de lièchē, xiànzài dàodá...hào zhàntái** 开往…的列车, 现在到达…号站台
The train from...is now arriving at platform...	**Cóng...kāichū de lièchē, xiànzài dàodá...hào zhàntái** 从…开出的列车, 现在到达…号站台
The train to...will leave from platform...	**Kāiwǎng... de lièchē, jiāng zài...hào zhàntái lízhàn** 开往…的列车, 将在…号站台离站
Today the [time] train to...will leave from platform...	**...diǎn kāiwǎng...de lièchē, jiāng zài...hào zhàntái lízhàn** …点开往…的列车, 将在…号站台离站
The next station is...	**Lièchē yùnxíng qiánfāng shì...zhàn** 列车运行前方是…站
Where does this train go to?	**Zhè cì lièchē kāiwǎng nǎli?** 这次列车开往哪里?
Does this train stop at...?	**Zhè cì lièchē zài...tíng ma?** 这次列车在…停吗?
Could you tell me where I have to get off for...?	**Qǐngwèn, wǒ dào...gāi zài nǎr xiàchē?** 请问, 我到…该在哪儿下车?

Could you let me know when we get to...?	**Dào...de shíhou, qǐng gàosu wǒ yì shēng** 到···的时候，请告诉我一声
Could you stop at the next stop, please?	**Máfan nín, xià ge zhàn wǒ xiàchē** 麻烦您，下个站我下车
Where are we?	**Wǒmen xiànzài zài nǎli?** 我们现在在哪里？
Can I get off the train for a while?	**Kěyǐ xiàchē kànkan ma?** 可以下车看看吗？
Do I have to get off here?	**Wǒ zài zhèlǐ xiàchē ma?** 我在这里下车吗？
Have we already passed...?	**Guòle...méiyǒu?** 过了···没有？
How long does the train stop here?	**Lièchē zài zhèlǐ tíng duō cháng shíjiān?** 列车在这里停多长时间？
Will we arrive on time?	**Wǒmen huì zhǔnshí dàodá ma?** 我们会准时到达吗？
Is this seat taken?	**Zhè ge wèizi yǒu rén zuò ma?** 这个位子有人坐吗？
Excuse me, this is my seat	**Duìbuqǐ, zhè shì wǒde wèizi** 对不起，这是我的位子

6.8 Long-distance trains

● **Train travel in China** is a good way to see the country. Long-distance trains are generally quite comfortable if you travel "soft class" (**ruǎnxí wòpù** 软席卧铺). The "soft class" car has a number of cabins each with four berths, a small table, and a sliding door. The "hard class" (**yìngxí wòpù** 硬席卧铺) is much less comfortable with six berths opening to a common walkway. There are toilets at the end of each car. Foreigners and Chinese business people generally take the more expensive but more comfortable "soft class." All train travelers are provided with free boiling water and they can order inexpensive meals.

Ticket types

What types of tickets would you like to buy?	**Nín xiǎng mǎi nǎ zhǒng piào?** 您想买哪种票?
Hard seat or soft seat?	**Yìngzuò háishi ruǎnzuò?** 硬座还是软座?
Hard berth or soft berth?	**Yìngwò háishi ruǎnwò?** 硬卧还是软卧?
There are three types of hard berths: top, middle or bottom	**Yìngwò yǒu sān zhǒng: shàngpù, zhōngpù hé xiàpù** 硬卧有三种: 上铺, 中铺和下铺
Which types of hard berths do you want: top, middle or bottom?	**Nǐ xiǎng yào shénme yìngwò: shàngpù, zhōngpù háishi xiàpù?** 你想要什么硬卧: 上铺, 中铺还是下铺?
There are two types of soft berths: top or bottom	**Ruǎnwò yǒu liǎng zhǒng: shàngpù hé xiàpù** 软卧有两种: 上铺和下铺
Which types of soft berths do you want: top or bottom?	**Nǐ xiǎng yào shénme ruǎnwò: shàngpù háishi xiàpù?** 你想要什么软卧: 上铺还是下铺?

Traveling by train

Destination	**mùdìdì** 目的地
Which city are you traveling to?	**Nǐ(men) qù nǎ ge chéngshì?** 你(们)去哪个城市?
When are you leaving?	**Nǐ(men) xiǎng shénme shíhou qù?** 你(们)想什么时候去?
Your train leaves at...	**Nǐ(men) de lièchē....kāi** 你(们)的列车 … 开
You have to change	**Nǐ(men) yào zhuǎnchē** 你(们)要转车
You have to get off at...	**Nǐ(men) yào zài...xiàchē** 你(们)要在 … 下车

Tickets, please	**Qǐng chūshì piào** 请出示票
Your reservation, please	**Qǐng bǎ nǐ yùdìng de piào gěi wǒ kànkan** 请把你预订的票给我看看
Your passport, please	**Qǐng bǎ nǐde hùzhào gěi wǒ kànkan** 请把你的护照给我看看
You're in the wrong seat	**Nǐ(men) zuòcuò wèizile** 你(们)坐错位子了
You have made a mistake	**Nǐ(men) nòngcuòle** 你(们)弄错了
This seat is reserved	**Zhè ge zuòr yǒu rén yùdìngle** 这个座儿有人预订了
You'll have to pay extra	**Nǐ(men) yào bǔpiào** 你(们)要补票
The...has been delayed by...minutes	**...wǎndiǎn...fēnzhōng** …晚点…分钟

6.9 Buses

Excuse me, which bus should I take to get to Wangfujing?	**Qǐngwèn, qù Wángfǔjǐng gāi zuò jǐlù gōnggòngqìchē?** 请问, 去王府井该坐几路公共汽车?
You can catch the 103 trolley bus	**Kěyǐ zuò yāolíngsān lù wúguǐdiànchē** 可以坐一零三路无轨电车
Excuse me, where should I change bus to get to the Australian Embassy?	**Qǐngwèn, qù Àozhōu dàshǐguǎn zài shénme dìfang huànchē?** 请问, 去澳洲大使馆在什么地方换车?
There's no need to change bus, take bus 318 till the terminal	**Búyào zhuǎnchē, nín zuò sānyāobā lù yīzhí dào zhōngdiǎn** 不要转车, 您坐三一八路一直到终点
We've arrived at Sun Yat-Sen Park. Passengers please get off now	**Zhōngshān gōngyuán dàole, qǐng xiàchē** 中山公园到了, 请下车

Next stop is Xidan, please get ready to get off	**Xià yí zhàn Xīdān, qǐng nín zhǔnbèi xiàchē** 下一站西单, 请您准备下车
Please let the passengers get off first to ensure safety	**Qǐng nín xiān-xià hòu-shàng, zhùyì ānquán** 请您先下后上, 注意安全
The bus is moving, please hold onto the hand grips	**Chē yào qǐdòng, qǐng lāhǎo fúshǒu** 车要起动, 请拉好扶手
What's the frequency of service for bus 101?	**Yāolíngyāo lù qìchē de chēcì duō bu duō?** 一零一路汽车的车次多不多?
The frequency of service for bus 101 is every 3 minutes	**Yāolíngyāo lù qìchē de chēcì hěnduō, měi sān fēnzhōng yí tàng** 一零一路汽车的车次很多, 每三分钟一趟
What's the earliest bus service for bus 107?	**Yāolíngqī lù qìchē de tóubānchē shì shénme shíjiān?** 一零七路汽车的头班车是什么时间?
The earliest bus service for bus 107 is 5:45 a.m.	**Yāolíngqī lù qìchē de tóubānchē shì zǎoshang wǔdiǎn sìshíwǔ fēn** 一零七路汽车的头班车是早上五点四十五分
What's the last bus service for bus 107?	**Yāolíngqī lù qìchē de mòbānchē shì shénme shíjiān?** 一零七路汽车的末班车是什么时间?
The last bus service for bus 107 is 11:30 p.m.	**Yāolíngqī lù qìchē de mòbānchē shì wǎnshang shíyīdiǎnbàn** 一零七路汽车的末班车是晚上十一点半

6.10 Taxis

● **Taxis** provide a reasonably priced and efficient means of getting about most of China's major cities. Taxis at hotels are generally more spacious and thus more expensive than those you hail on the street. You may want to ask your driver (**sījī** 司机) to wait for you while you are on sightseeing trips or finishing your business as waiting time is not expensive. It's an excellent idea to ask someone to write down your destination in characters before you take a taxi.

You can also rent your own taxi with its driver for a day or two. This is a good way to see a lot of the sights at your own pace. Price is negotiable with the driver. If you can split the cost with your companions, the price is generally reasonable.

出租 **chūzū** for hire	有人 **yǒurén** occupied	出租汽车站 **chūzū qìchēzhàn** taxi stand

Taxi!	**Chūzūchē!** 出租车！
Could you get me a taxi please?	**Qǐng bāng wǒ jiào yí liàng chūzūchē** 请帮我叫一辆出租车
Where can I find a taxi around here?	**Nǎli yǒu chūzūchē?** 哪里有出租车？
Could you take me to..., please?	**Qǐng dài wǒ dào...** 请带我到…
Could you take me to this address, please	**Qǐng dài wǒ dào zhè ge dìzhǐ** 请带我到这个地址
– to the...hotel, please	**Qǐng dài wǒ dào... bīn'guǎn/lǚguǎn** 请带我到…宾馆／旅馆
– to the town/city center, please	**Qǐng dài wǒ dào...chénglǐ** 请带我到…城里
– to the station, please	**Qǐng dài wǒ dào...huǒchēzhàn** 请带我到…火车站
– to the airport, please	**Qǐng dài wǒ dào... jīchǎng** 请带我到…机场
How much is the trip to...?	**Qù... duōshao qiǎn?** 去…多少钱？
How far is it to...?	**Zhèlǐ lí... yǒu duō yuǎn?** 这里离…有多远？

Could you turn on the meter, please (driver)?	**Sījī, qǐng nǐ dǎbiǎo** 司机，请你打表
I'm in a hurry	**Wǒ zài gǎn shíjiān** 我在赶时间
Could you speed up/ slow down a little?	**Néng kāi de kuài/màn yìdiǎn ma?** 能开得快／慢一点吗？
Could you take a different route?	**Néng zǒu lìng yì tiáo lù ma?** 能走另一条路吗？
I'd like to get out here, please	**Wǒ zài zhèlǐ xiàchē** 我在这里下车
I'd like to rent a Japanese car	**Wǒ yào zū yí liàng Rìběnchē** 我要租一辆日本车
How much does it cost to hire ... ?	**Zū...yào duōshao qián?** 租…要多少钱？
– per day	**yì tiān** 一天
– two days	**liǎng tiān** 两天
– per kilometer	**yì gōnglǐ** 一公里
How many kilometers per day do I get for the basic fee?	**Měitiān de jīběn fèiyòng néng bàoxiāo duōshao gōnglǐ?** 每天的基本费用能报销多少公里？
Does the price include gas?	**Jiàqián bāokuò qìyóu fèi ma?** 价钱包括汽油费吗？
Can the driver speak English?	**Sījī huì shuō Yīngyǔ ma?** 司机会说英语吗？
Will the driver stay with me all day?	**Sījī zhěngtiān dōu péizhe wǒ ma?** 司机整天都陪着我吗？
Shall I take care of the driver's meals?	**Wǒ yào fùzé sījī de fànqián ma?** 我要负责司机的饭钱吗？
Do I settle the cost with the driver at the end of the day?	**Wǒ zài yì tiān jié shù shí gēn sījī jiézhàng ma?** 我在一天结束时跟司机结账吗？

Go …	**Zǒu ba** 走吧
You have to go...here	**Yào cóng zhèlǐ...qù** 要从这里…去
Go straight ahead	**Yìzhí zǒu** 一直走
Turn left	**Zhuǎn zuǒ** 转左
Turn right	**Zhuǎn yòu** 转右
This is it/We're here	**Zhèlǐ jiù shì/Dàole** 这里就是 / 到了
Could you wait a minute for me, please?	**Nǐ néng děng wǒ yíhuìr ma?** 你能等我一会儿吗？
How much do I owe you?	**Wǒ gāi fù nǐ duōshao qián?** 我该付你多少钱？

7 A Place to Stay

7.1 General   106

7.2 Hotels/hostels/budget
accommodations   107

7.3 Requests   111

7.4 Complaints   113

7.5 Departure   115

7. A Place to Stay

7.1 General

● **In China**, hotels for foreigners range from the basic two-star twin share accommodation with own bathroom (**lǚguǎn** 旅馆) in small towns and outlying areas to five-star accommodations (**bīn'guǎn/fàndiàn** 宾馆／饭店) with swimming pools, sauna, restaurants etc. in capital cities. Hotels around railway stations generally cater mainly for Chinese travelers with sub-standard accommodation (**zhāodàisuǒ** 招待所). Increasingly there are youth hotels for foreign backpackers in major cities such as Beijing.

I'm looking for a cheap/good hotel	**Wǒ yào zhǎo yì jiā piányi de/hǎo de lǚguǎn** 我要找一家便宜的／好的旅馆
I'm looking for a nearby hotel	**Wǒ yào zhǎo yì jiā línjìn de lǚguǎn** 我要找一家邻近的旅馆
Do you give discounts for students?	**Nǐmen duì liúxuéshēng yǒu méiyǒu yōuhuì?** 你们对留学生有没有优惠？
I'm not sure how long I'm staying	**Wǒ hái bù zhīdao yào zhù duō jiǔ** 我还不知道要住多久
Do you have any rooms?	**Nǐmen yǒu méiyǒu kōng fáng?** 你们有没有空房？
Do you have air-conditioning/heating in the room?	**Fángjiān lǐ yǒu méiyǒu kōngtiáo/nuǎnqì?** 房间里有没有空调／暖气？
Do you have hot water all day?	**Nǐmen zhěng tiān dōu yǒu rèshuǐ ma?** 你们整天都有热水吗？
When is the heating turned on?	**Shénme shíhou cái kāi nuǎnqì?** 什么时候才开暖气？
Do you have room service?	**Nǐmen yǒu méiyǒu kèfáng fúwù?** 你们有没有客房服务？

Where's the emergency exit/fire escape?	**Jǐnjí/ánquán chūkǒu zài nǎr?** 紧急／安全出口在哪儿？
The key to room…, please	**Qǐng gěi wǒ…hào fángjiān de yàoshi** 请给我…号房间的钥匙
Could you put this in the safe, please?	**Qǐng bǎ zhège dōngxi fàng zài bǎoxiǎnxiāng lǐ** 请把这个东西放在保险箱里
Could you wake me at…tomorrow?	**Míngtiān qǐng zài…diǎn jiàoxǐng wǒ** 明天请在…点叫醒我
Could I have an extra blanket?	**Kěyǐ zài gěi wǒ yì chuáng tǎnzi ma?** 可以再给我一床毯子吗？
What time does the gate/door open/close?	**Dàmén jǐ diǎnzhōng kāi/guān?** 大门几点钟开／关？
Could you get me a taxi, please?	**Qǐng gěi wǒ jiào yí liàng chūchūchē, hǎo ma?** 请给我叫一辆出租车，好吗？
Could you find a babysitter for me?	**Kěyǐ gěi wǒ zhǎo ge línshí bǎomǔ ma?** 可以给我找个临时保姆吗？
Is there any mail for me?	**Yǒu méiyǒu wǒde xìn?** 有没有我的信？

A Place to Stay

请填这张表格 **Qǐng tián zhè zhāng biǎogé**	Fill out this form, please
请给我看看你的护照 **Qǐng gěi wǒ kànkan nǐde hùzhào**	Could I see your passport?
你需要交押金 **Nǐ xūyào jiāo yājīn**	You need to put a deposit

Hotels/hostels/budget accommodations

Booking

My name is…	**Wǒde míngzi shì…** 我的名字是…

I've made a reservation	**Wǒ yǐjiīng yùdìngle fángjiān** 我已经预订了房间
I wrote to you last month	**Wǒ zài shàng ge yuè gěi nǐmen xiěguo xìn** 我在上个月给你们写过信
Here's the confirmation	**Zhè shì quèrèndān** 这是确认单
How much is it per night/week?	**Wǒ zhù de fángjiān duōshao qián yì tiān/yì (ge) xīngqī?** 我住的房间多少钱一天／一（个）星期？
We'll be staying for... nights/weeks	**Wǒmen dǎsuàn zhù...tiān/(ge) xīngqī** 我们打算住…天／（个）星期
I'd like a single/double room	**Wǒ yào yì jiān dānrénfáng/shuāngrénfáng** 我要一间单人房／双人房
per person/per room	**yí ge rén/yì jiān fáng** 一个人／一间房
I'd like a room with...	**Wǒ yào yī jiān yǒu...de fángjiān** 我要一间有…的房间
twin beds	**liǎng zhāng chuáng** 两张床
a double bed	**yì zhāng shuāngrénchuáng** 一张双人床
a bath tub	**yùpén** 浴盆
a shower	**línyù** 淋浴
a balcony	**yángtái** 阳台
a suite	**yì jiān tàofáng** 一间套房
Could we have adjoining rooms?	**Wǒmen néng bu néng zhù gébì?** 我们能不能住隔壁？

We'd like a room...	**Wǒmen yào yì jiān...fáng**
	我们要一间…房
facing the front	**cháo qiān de**
	朝前的
at the back	**cháo hòu de**
	朝后的
with street/river/ sea view	**miànduì dàjiē/hé/hǎi de**
	面对大街／河／海的
Does that include breakfast/lunch/dinner?	**Fángjià bāokuò zǎocān/wǔcan/ wǎncān ma?**
	房价包括早餐／午餐／晚餐吗？
Is there...in the room?	**Fángjiān lǐ yǒu méiyǒu...?**
	房间里有没有…？
air conditioning/heating	**kōngtiáo/nuǎnqì**
	空调／暖气
TV	**diànshìjī**
	电视机
refrigerator	**diànbīngxiāng**
	电冰箱
hot water	**rèshuǐ**
	热水
electric jug	**diànshuǐhú**
	电水壶

Hotels/motels

Could I see the room?	**Wǒ néng kànkan fángjiān ma?**
	我能看看房间吗？
We don't like this one	**Wǒmen bù xǐhuan zhè jiān**
	我们不喜欢这间
Do you have another room?	**Hái yǒu biéde fángjiān ma?**
	还有别的房间吗？
Do you have a larger room?	**Yǒu dàyìdiǎnde fángjiān ma?**
	有大一点的房间吗？

Do you have a less expensive room?	**Yǒu gèng piányi de fángjiān ma?** 有更便宜的房间吗?
We prefer a quiet room	**Wǒmen xǐhuan ānjìng de fángjiān** 我们喜欢安静的房间
No, they are all occupied	**Méiyǒu le, dōu zhùmǎn le** 没有了，都住满了
This room is too...	**Zhè fángjiān tài...le** 这房间太…了
hot/cold	**rè/lěng** 热 / 冷
dark/small	**àn/xiǎo** 暗 / 小
noisy	**cáozá** 嘈杂
I'll take this room	**Wǒ jiù yào zhè ge fángjiān** 我就要这个房间
Could you put in a cot?	**Néng jiā fàng yì zhāng yīng'érchuáng ma?** 能加放一张婴儿床吗?
What time's breakfast?	**Jǐ diǎn chī zǎocān?** 几点吃早餐?
Where's the dining room?	**Cāntīng zài nǎlǐ?** 餐厅在哪里?
Can I have breakfast in my room?	**Kěyǐ zài fángjiān lǐ chī zǎocān ma?** 可以在房间里吃早餐吗?

请跟我来
Qǐng gēn wǒ lái

This way please

你的房间在…层 / 楼，…号房间
Nǐ de fángjiān zài... céng/lóu, ...hào fángjiān

Your room is on the...floor, number...

厕所和淋浴室在同一层 / 房间
Cèsuǒ hé línyù shì zài tóngyīcéng/ fángjiān

The toilet and shower are on the same floor/in the room

How much is the room per night?	**Zhè zhǒng fángjiān duōshao qián yì wǎn?** 这种房间多少钱一晚？
Does this include...	**Zhè ge fángjià shìfǒu bāokuò...?** 这个房价是否包括…？
breakfast	**zǎocān** 早餐
three meals	**sāncān** 三餐
service	**fúwùfèi** 服务费

7.3 Requests

I need a two-prong plug	**Wǒ xūyào yí ge shuāngxiàn chātóu** 我需要一个双线插头
I need a three-prong plug	**Wǒ xūyào yí ge sānxiàn chātóu** 我需要一个三线插头
I need this kind of plug	**Wǒ xūyào zhè zhǒng chātóu** 我需要这种插头
Where's the plug for the razor?	**Guāhúdāo de chāzuò zài nǎli?** 刮胡刀的插座在哪里？
What's the voltage?	**Zhèlǐ de diànyā shì duōshao fú?** 这里的电压是多少伏？
May I have...?	**Néng bu néng gěi wǒ...?** 能不能给我…？
(more) hangers	**...ge yījià** …个衣架
a needle and some thread	**yì gén zhén hé yìxiē xiàn** 一根针和一些线
(more) blankets	**... tiáo tǎnzi** …条毯子
(another) pillow	**(zài ná yí ge) zhěntou** （再拿一个）枕头

some stationery	**xìnzhǐ** 信纸
soap	**féizào** 肥皂
shampoo	**xǐfàjì** 洗发剂
bath lotion	**xǐzǎoyè** 洗澡液
bath towel	**yùjīn** 浴巾
cold drinking water	**liáng kāishuǐ** 凉开水
hot drinking water	**rè kāishuǐ** 热开水
Can you repair this...?	**Nǐ néng bu néng bāng wǒ dàixiū zhè...** 你能不能帮我代修这…
camera	**zhàoxiàngjī** 照相机
video camera	**shèxiàngjī** 摄相机
suitcase	**xiāngzi** 箱子
The room needs to be cleaned	**Néng bu néng dǎsǎo yíxià wǒ de fángjiān?** 能不能打扫一下我的房间？
Please change the sheets/towels	**Qǐng huàn yíxià chuángdān/máojīn** 请换一下床单 / 毛巾
Please send my breakfast/lunch/ dinner to my room	**Qǐng bǎ zǎocān/wǔcān/wǎncān sòngdào wǒde fángjiān lǐ** 请把早餐／午餐／晚餐送到我的房间里
I'd like these clothes...	**Qǐng bǎ zhèxiē yīfu...** 请把这些衣服…
washed	**xǐgānjìng** 洗干净

ironed	**yùnhǎo** 熨好
dry-cleaned	**gānxǐ** 干洗
I'm leaving tonight. Can I put my laundry in?	**Wǒ jīntiān wǎnshang zǒu, hái néng xǐ yīfu ma?** 我今天晚上走，还能洗衣服吗？
Is my laundry ready?	**Wǒde yīfu xǐhǎole ma?** 我的衣服洗好了吗？
I need it at...	**Wǒ yào...qǔ** 我要…取
today	**jīntiān** 今天
tonight	**jīnwǎn** 今晚
tomorrow	**míngtiān** 明天
I want it as soon as possible	**Wǒ xīwàng néng yuè kuài yuè hǎo** 我希望能越快越好
Can you sew on this button?	**Qǐng gěi wǒ féng yí ge kòuzi** 请给我缝一个扣子
This isn't mine	**Zhè bú shì wǒde** 这不是我的
There is one piece missing	**Wǒ shǎole yí jiàn yīfu** 我少了一件衣服
I'm leaving soon, but my laundry is not back yet	**Wǒ yào zǒu le, xǐ de yīfu hái méiyǒu sònglái ne** 我要走了，洗的衣服还没有送来呢

7.4 Complaints

We can't sleep for the noise	**Shēngyīn tài cáozá le, wǒmen shuìbuzháo** 声音太嘈杂了，我们睡不着

Could you turn the radio down, please?	**Qǐng tiáodī yíxià shōuyīnjī** 请调低一下收音机
We're out of toilet paper	**Shǒuzhǐ/wèishēngzhǐ yòngwánle** 手纸 / 卫生纸用完了
There aren't any.../ there's not enough...	**Méiyǒu... le/...búgòu** 没有…了 / …不够
The bed linen's dirty	**Chuángdān shì zāng de** 床单是脏的
The room hasn't been cleaned	**Fángjiān méiyǒu shōushí** 房间没有收拾
The heating isn't working	**Nuǎnqì yǒu wèntí, búrè** 暖气有问题, 不热
There's no (hot) water/ electricity	**Méiyǒu (rè) shuǐ/diàn** 没有(热)水 / 电
...doesn't work/is broken	**...yǒu máobìng/huài le** …有毛病 / 坏了
The toilet is blocked	**Cèsuǒ dǔsè le** 厕所堵塞了
The sink is blocked	**Shuǐcáo dǔsè le** 水槽堵塞了
The tap is dripping	**Shuǐlóngtóu lòushuǐ le** 水龙头漏水了
The bulb is burnt out	**Déngpào huài le** 灯泡坏了
The blind is broken	**Bǎiyèchuāng lābudòng le** 百叶窗拉不动了
Could you have that seen to?	**Qǐng nín zhǎo rén xiū yíxià** 请您找人修一下
Could I have another room?	**Wǒ kěyǐ lìng yào yì jiān fángjiān ma?** 我可以另要一间房间吗?
The bed creaks terribly	**Chuáng xiǎngde lìhai** 床响得厉害
The bed sags	**Chuáng huì āoxiàqù** 床会凹下去

It's too noisy	**Zhèr tài chǎo le**
	这儿太吵了
This place is full of mosquitos	**Zhèlǐ dàochù dōu shì wénzi**
	这里到处都是蚊子
– cockroaches	**zhāngláng**
	蟑螂

7.5 Departure

See also 8.2 Settling the bill

I'm leaving (the hotel) tomorrow	**Wǒ míngtiān líkāi (lǚdiàn)**
	我明天离开（旅店）
Where can I pay my bill, please?	**Qǐngwèn, wǒ dào nǎli fù fángfèi?**
	请问，我到哪里付房费？
My room number is...	**Wǒde fánghào shì...**
	我的房号是…
What time should we check out?	**Wǒmen yīnggāi jǐdiǎn bàn lídiàn shǒuxù?**
	我们应该几点办离店手续？
I'm leaving early tomorrow. Please prepare the bill	**Wǒ míngtiān hěn zǎo jiù yào zǒu, qǐng zhǔnbèihǎo zhàngdān**
	我明天很早就要走，请准备好账单
Could I have my deposit back, please?	**Qǐng huán gěi wǒ yājīn**
	请还给我押金
I must leave at once	**Wǒ bìxū mǎshàng líkāi**
	我必须马上离开
Is this my bill?	**Zhè shì wǒde zhàngdān ma?**
	这是我的账单吗？
Is everything included?	**Suǒyǒu fèiyòng dōu bāokuò le ma?**
	所有费用都包括了吗？
Do you accept credit cards?	**Nǐmen jiēshòu xìnyòngkǎ ma?**
	你们接受信用卡吗？

(I reckon) you've made a mistake in the bill

Wǒ rènwéi zhàngdān shàng yǒu yí chù cuòwù

我认为账单上有一处错误

Could you forward my mail to this address?

Qǐng bǎ wǒde yóujiàn jìdào zhè ge dìzhǐ

请把我的邮件寄到这个地址

Could I leave my luggage here until I leave?

Xíngli liú zài zhèlǐ děng wǒ zǒu yǐqián zài qǔ, kěyǐ ma?

行李留在这里等我走以前再取, 可以吗?

Thanks for your hospitality

Gǎnxiè nǐmende rèqíng zhāodài

感谢你们的热情招待

We enjoyed it, thank you

Wǒmen zhùde hěn mǎnyì, xièxie

我们住得很满意, 谢谢

8 Money Matters

8.1 Banks   118

8.2 Settling the bill   120

8. Money Matters

● **In general**, banks are open Monday to Friday from 9 a.m. to 5 p.m., but it is always possible to exchange money in hotels or other tourist centers. Your passport is usually needed to do so.

8.1 Banks

Where can I change foreign currency?	**Shàng nǎr kěyǐ huàn wàibì?** 上哪儿可以换外币？
Where can I find the Bank of China around here?	**Zhèlǐ nǎli yǒu Zhōngguó Yínháng?** 这里哪里有中国银行？
Where can I cash this traveler's check?	**Nǎli kěyǐ duìhuàn lǚxíng zhīpiào?** 哪里可以兑换旅行支票？
Can I cash this traveler's check here?	**Kěyǐ zài zhèlǐ duìhuàn lǚxíng zhīpiào ma?** 可以在这里兑换旅行支票吗？
What's today's exchange rate for...?	**Jīntiān...duìhuàn...de duìhuànlǜ shì duōshao?** 今天…兑换…的兑换率是多少？
– US dollars	**Měiyuán** 美元
– English pounds	**Yīngbàng** 英镑
– Japanese Yen	**Rìyuán** 日元
– Australian dollars	**Àobì/Àoyuán** 澳币／澳元
– Hong Kong dollars	**Gǎngbì** 港币
Can I withdraw money on my credit card here?	**Kěyǐ zài zhèlǐ yòng xìnyòngkǎ qǔqián ma?** 可以在这里用信用卡取钱吗？

What's the maximum amount?	**Yí cì zuìduō kěyǐ qǔ duōshao qián?** 一次最多可以取多少钱？
What's the minimum amount?	**Yí cì zuìshǎo yào qǔ duōshao qián?** 一次最少要取多少钱？
I had some money cabled here	**Yǒu rén gěi wǒ diànhuìle yìdiǎn qián lái** 有人给我电汇了一点钱来
I'm expecting some money from…	**Wǒ zhèngzài děng cóng...huìlái de qián** 我正在等从…汇来的钱
These are the details of my bank in the US	**Zhè shì wǒ zài Měiguó de yínháng zīliào** 这是我在美国的银行资料
This is the number of my bank account	**Zhè shì wǒ de yínháng zhànghào** 这是我的银行账号
Could you write it down for me?	**Nǐ néng bu néng xiěxiàlái gěi wǒ?** 你能不能写下来给我？
I'd like to change some money	**Wǒ yào duìhuàn wàibì** 我要兑换外币
Could you give me some small change with it?	**Qǐng gěi wǒ yìxiē língqián** 请给我一些零钱
This is not right	**Zhè ge búduì** 这个不对

请签名 **Qǐng qiānmíng**	Sign here, please
请填这张表 **Qǐng tián zhè zhāng biǎo**	Fill this out, please
请给我看看你的护照 **Qǐng gěi wǒ kànkan nǐde hùzhào**	Could I see your passport, please?
请给我看看你的身份证 **Qǐng gěi wǒ kànkan nǐde shēnfènzhèng**	Could I see your identity card, please?
请给我看看你的信用卡 **Qǐng gěi wǒ kànkan nǐde xìnyòngkǎ**	Could I see your credit card, please?

8.2 Settling the bill

Could you put it on my bill?	**Qǐng jì zài wǒde zhàngdān shàng** 请记在我的账单上
Is everything included?	**Dōu suànjìnqu le ma?** 都算进去了吗?
Is the tip included?	**Xiǎofèi yě bāokuò le ma?** 小费也包括了吗?
Can I pay by credit card?	**Wǒ kěyǐ yòng xìnyòngkǎ fùkuǎn ma?** 我可以用信用卡付款吗?
Can I pay by traveler's check?	**Wǒ kěyǐ yòng lǚxíng zhīpiào fùkuǎn ma?** 我可以用旅行支票付款吗?
Can I pay with foreign currency?	**Wǒ kěyǐ yòng wàibì fùkuǎn ma?** 我可以用外币付款吗?
You've given me too much change	**Nǐ zhǎo gěi wǒ de qián tài duō le** 你找给我的钱太多了
You haven't given me enough change	**Nǐ zhǎo gěi wǒ de qián bú gòu** 你找给我的钱不够
Could you check this again, please?	**Qǐng nǐ zài suànyisuàn** 请你再算一算
Could I have a receipt, please?	**Qǐng gěi wǒ shōujù** 请给我收据
This is for you	**Zhè shì gěi nǐ de xiǎofèi** 这是给你的小费
Keep the change	**Búyòng zhǎo le** 不用找了

| (对不起), 我们不接信用卡 /
旅行支票 / 外币
**(Duìbùqǐ), wǒmen bù jiē
xìnyòngkǎ/lǚxíng zhīpiào/wàibì** | We don't accept credit cards/
traveler's checks/foreign currency |

9 Mail, Phone and Internet

9.1	Mail	122
9.2	Telephone	124
9.3	Internet/email	126

9. Mail, Phone and Internet

9.1 Mail

● **Post offices are open Monday to Saturday** from 8:30 a.m. to 6 p.m. In fact, some post offices stay open until 9 p.m. although the range of services decreases towards late evening. The opening hours for Sundays are from 8:30 a.m. to 6 p.m. The cost of sending a letter depends on its weight, thus the many queues for weighing letters and the buying of stamps of various values.

邮票
yóupiào
stamps
	电汇/(邮政／银行)汇票
	diànhuì/(yóuzhèng/
	  yínháng) huìpiào
	money orders
	
	挂号邮件
	guàhào yóujiàn
	registered mail
		包裹
		bāoguǒ
		parcels
		
		明信片
		míngxìnpiàn
		postcard
			保价邮件
			bǎojià yóujiàn
			insured mail/
			  post
			
			快递
			kuàidì
			express mail

Where is…?
…zài nǎr/nǎli?
… 在哪儿／哪里？

– the nearest post office
zuìkàojìn de yóujú
最靠近的邮局

– the main post office
yóujú zǒngjú
邮局总局

– the nearest mail box
zuìjìnde yóuxiāng
最近的邮箱

Which counter should
  I go to…?
Wǒ yīnggāi qù nǎ ge guìtái…?
我应该去哪个柜台…？

Which counter should I
  go to to send a fax?
Wǒ yīnggāi qù nǎ ge guìtái fā
chuánzhēn?
我应该去哪个柜台发传真？

Which counter should I go
  to wire a money order?
Wǒ yīnggāi qù nǎ ge guìtái fā diànhuì?
我应该去哪个柜台发电汇？

| Which counter should I go to for general delivery? | **Wǒ yīnggāi qù nǎ ge guìtái qǔ yóujiàn?**
我应该去哪个柜台取邮件? |
| Is there any mail for me? | **Yǒu méiyǒu wǒde xìn?**
有没有我的信? |

Stamps

What's the postage for a letter/postcard to...?	**Jì xìn/míngxìnpiàn dào...de yóufèi shì duōshao?** 寄信 / 明信片到…的邮费是多少?
Are there enough stamps on it?	**Yóupiào gòu bu gòu?** 邮票够不够?
I'd like [quantity] [value] stamps	**Wǒ yào [...zhāng] [...qián] de yóupiào** 我要(…张)(…钱)的邮票
I'd like to send this...	**Wǒ xiǎng jì...** 我想寄…
– express	**kuàiyóu** 快邮
– by air mail	**hángkōng** 航空
– by registered mail	**guàhào** 挂号
– by surface mail	**hǎiyùn** 海运

Fax

I'd like to send a fax to...	**Wǒ xiǎng fā chuánzhēn dào...** 我想发传真到…
Can I make photocopies/send a fax here?	**Zhèlǐ kěyǐ fùyìn/fā chuánzhēn ma?** 这里可以复印 / 发传真吗?
How much is it per page?	**Duōshao qián yí yè?** 多少钱一页?

9.2 Telephone

● **Direct international calls** can be made from public telephones using a phone card available from shops, newspaper stands and post offices. Phone cards have a value of RMB50–RMB200. Dial 00 to get out of China, then the relevant country code (USA 1), city code and number. To find a telephone number in Beijing, you can look up the yellow pages. To dial direct, ring 114 locally. All operators speak English. When phoning someone in China, you will be greeted with **Nǐ hǎo** 你好.

Is there a phone booth around here?	**Fùjìn yǒu gōngyòng diànhuàtíng ma?** 附近有公用电话亭吗?
May I use your phone, please?	**Wǒ kěyǐ jièyòng nǐde diànhuà ma?** 我可以借用你的电话吗?
Do you have a (city/region) phone directory?	**Yǒu méiyǒu (běnshì/běnqū) de diànhuàbù?** 有没有(本市／本区)的电话簿?
Where can I get a phone card?	**Nǎli kěyǐ mǎi diànhuàkǎ?** 哪里可以买电话卡?
Could you give me…?	**Qǐng gěi wǒ chá yíxià…** 请给我查一下…
– the number of room…?	**…hào fángjiān de diànhuà hàomǎ** …号房间的电话号码
– the number for international directory assistance?	**guójì diànhuà fúwùchù de hàomǎ** 国际电话服务处的号码
– the international access code?	**guójì chángtú de hàomǎ** 国际长途的号码
– the country code?	**guójiā dàihào** 国家代号
– the area code for…?	**…de dìqūhào** …的地区号
Can I dial international (long distance) direct?	**Wǒ kěyǐ zhíjiē dǎ guójì chángtú ma?** 我可以直接打国际长途吗?

Do I have to reserve my calls?	**Dǎ diànhuà yào yùdìng shíjiān ma?** 打电话要预订时间吗？
Could you dial this number for me, please?	**Qǐng gěi wǒ dǎ zhè ge diànhuà hàomǎ** 请给我打这个电话号码
I'd like to place a collect call to…	**Wǒ xiǎng dìng yí gè (chángtú) diànhuà. Yào duìfāng fùkuǎn de** 我想订一个（长途）电话。要对方付款的
Have there been any calls for me?	**Yǒu méiyǒu rén gěi wǒ dǎguo diànhuà?** 有没有人给我打过电话？

The conversation

Hello, this is…	**Wèi/Wéi, zhè shì…** 喂，这是…
Who is this, please?	**Qǐngwèn, nín shì shéi/Nín něi/nǎ wèi?** 请问，您是谁／您哪位？
Is this…?	**Nín/Nǐ shì …ma?** 您／你是…吗？
I'm sorry, I've dialed the wrong number	**Duìbuqǐ, wǒ dǎcuò le** 对不起，我打错了
I can't hear you	**Wǒ tīng bu qīngchu** 我听不清楚
I'd like to speak to…	**Wǒ zhǎo…/…zài bu zài?** 我找… ／ …在不在？
Is there anybody who speaks English?	**Nǐmen yǒu rén huì jiǎng Yìngyǔ ma?** 你们有人会讲英语吗？
Extension…, please	**Qǐng jiē…fēnjì** 请接…分机
Could you ask him/her to call me back?	**Qǐng ràng tā gěi wǒ huí ge diànhuà** 请让他／她给我回个电话
My name's…	**Wǒ jiào…** 我叫…
My number's…	**Wǒ de diànhuà hàomǎ shì…** 我的电话号码是…

Could you tell him/
her I called?

Qǐng gàosu tā, wǒ gěi tā dǎguo diànhuà
请告诉他／她，我给他／她打过电话

I'll call him/her back
tomorrow

Wǒ míngtiān zài gěi tā huí diànhuà
我明天再给他／她回电话

你有电话
Nǐ yǒu diànhuà

There's a phone call for you

你要先拨"零"
Nǐ yào xiān bō "líng"

You have to dial "0" first

请等一等
Qǐng děng yì děng

One moment, please

没人接
Méi rén jiē

There's no answer

电话占线
Diànhuà zhànxiàn

The line's busy

您要等一下吗?
Nín yào děng yíxià ma?

Do you want to hold?

现在给你接
Xiànzài gěi nǐ jiē

Connecting you

你打错了
Nǐ dǎ cuòle

You've got a wrong number

他／她不在
Tā bù zài

He's/She's not here right now

他／她…点回来
Tā…diǎn huílái

He'll/she'll be back at…

9.3 Internet/email

网吧	伊妹儿	博客	聊天软件
wǎngbā	**yīmèiér**	**bókè**	**liáotiān ruǎnjiàn**
Internet café	email	blog	instant messenger

What is your email
address?

Nǐ de diànzǐyóujiàn dìzhǐ shì shénme?
你的电子邮件地址是什么?

My email address is…	**Wǒde diànzǐyóujiàn dìzhǐ shì...** 我的电子邮件地址是…
Could you send me an email?	**Kěyǐ qǐng nǐ fā diànzǐyóujiàn gěi wǒ ma?** 可以请你发电子邮件给我吗?
I will get back to you via email	**Wǒ huì fā diànzǐyóujiàn huífù nǐ** 我会发电子邮件回复你
Could you forward the email to Mr. Lin?	**Kěyǐ qǐng nǐ jiāng zhèfēng yóujiàn zhuǎnfā gěi Lín xiānsheng ma?** 可以请你将这封邮件转发给林先生吗?
Please reply the email as soon as possible	**Qǐng nǐ jǐnkuài huífù zhèfēng yóujiàn** 请你尽快回复这封邮件
I will be online from 8:00 a.m. to 5:00 p.m.	**Wǒ cóng shàngwǔ bādiǎn dào xiàwǔ wǔdiǎn huì zàixiànshàng** 我从上午八点到下午五点会在线上
We can chat on online	**Wǒmen kěyǐ zàixiànshàng liáotiān** 我们可以在线上聊天
What time is the video conference?	**Shìpínhuìyì shì jǐdiǎn?** 视频会议是几点?
Give me a second. I am logging in	**Děngwǒyíxià. Wǒ xiànzài dēnglù** 等我一下。我现在登录
The Internet connection is bad/unstable/ slow	**Wǎngluò liánjiē bùhǎo/bùwěndìng/ hěnmàn** 网络连接不好 / 不稳定 / 很慢

10 Shopping

10.1 Shopping conversations   130

10.2 Food   132

10.3 Clothing and shoes   133

10.4 At the hairdresser   135

10. Shopping

● **Most shops in China** are open seven days a week. Corner shops are open from 8:30 a.m. till 10 p.m. Supermarkets are open from 8:30 a.m. till 8:30 p.m., some places up to 9 p.m. Department stores are open from 9/10 a.m. till 9 p.m., some places up to 10 p.m.

超(级)市(场)
chāo (jí) shì (chǎng)
supermarket

百货公司
bǎihuò gōngsī
department store

水果蔬菜店
shuǐguǒ shūcàidiàn
fruit and vegetable shop

杂货店
záhuòdiàn
grocery shop

花店
huādiàn
florist

市场
shìchǎng
market

鱼店
yúdiàn
fishmonger

鸡店
jīdiàn
poultry shop

肉店
ròudiàn
butcher's shop

家庭用品店
jiātíng yòngpǐn diàn
household goods

家用电器店
jiāyòng diànqìdiàn
household appliances
 (white goods)

床单桌布店
chuángdān zhuōbùdiàn
household linen shop

服饰店
fúshìdiàn
costume jewelry shop

乐器店
yuèqìdiàn
musical instrument
 shop

男子服饰用品店
**nánzǐ fúshì yòngpǐn
 diàn**
haberdashery

钟表店
zhōngbiǎo diàn
watches and clocks

皮货商 / 皮货店
píhuòshāng/píhuòdiàn
furrier

眼镜商
yǎnjìngshāng
optician

服装店
fúzhuāngdiàn
clothing shop

理发店
lǐfàdiàn
barber's

理发师 / 理发店
lǐfàshī/lǐfàdiàn
hairdresser

香水店
xiāngshuǐdiàn
perfumery

鞋店
xiédiàn
footwear

皮革用品(店)
pígé yòngpǐn (diàn)
leather goods

中药店
zhōngyàodiàn
herbalist's shop

药店
yàodiàn
pharmacy

修鞋店
xiūxiédiàn
cobbler

烟草商
yāncǎoshāng
tobacconist

金饰工
jīnshìgōng
goldsmith

珠宝商
zhūbǎoshāng
jeweler

美容店
měiróngdiàn
beauty salon

洗衣店
xǐyīdiàn
laundry

投币洗衣店 / 干洗店
tóu bì xǐyīdiàn/gānxǐdiàn
coin-operated laundry/
 dry cleaner

面包店
miànbāodiàn
baker's shop

糖果店 / 糕点店
tángguǒdiàn/gāodiǎndiàn
confectioner's/cake shop

冰激凌店 / 冰淇淋店
bīngjīlíngdiàn/
 bīngqílíndiàn
ice-cream stand

欧式副食店
ōushì fùshídiàn
delicatessen

照相机店
zhàoxiàngjīdiàn
camera shop

文具店
wénjùdiàn
stationery shop

运动用品(店)
yùndòng yòngpǐn (diàn)
sporting goods

书店
shūdiàn
bookshop

玩具店
wánjùdiàn
toy shop

报亭
bàotíng
newsstand

摩托车 / 助动车 /
 自行车维修店
mótuōchē/
 zhùdòngchē/
 zìxíngchē
 wéixiūdiàn
motorbike/moped/
 bicycle repairs

音响店
yīnxiǎngdiàn
music shop (CDs,
 tapes, etc)

10.1 Shopping conversations

Where can I get…?	**Nǎli kěyǐ mǎidào…?** 哪里可以买到…?
When is this shop open?	**Zhè jiā shāngdiàn jǐdiǎn kāimén?** 这家商店几点开门?
Could you tell me where the…department is?	**Bùhǎoyìsi, …bùmén zài nǎli?** 不好意思, …部门在哪里?
Could you help me, please?	**Bùhǎoyìsi, néng máfan nǐ yíxià ma?** 不好意思, 能麻烦你一下吗?
I'm looking for…	**Wǒ zhǎo…** 我找…
Do you sell English language newspapers?	**Nǐmen yǒu Yīngwén bào ma?** 你们有英文报吗?

你有人招呼了吗?
Nǐ yǒurén zhāohū le ma?

Are you being served?

No, I'd like…

Hái méiyǒu, wǒ xiǎng mǎi...
还没有, 我想买…

I'm just looking, if that's all right

Wǒ zhǐshì kànkan, kěyǐ ma?
我只是看看, 可以吗?

还要别的吗?
Hái yào bié de ma?

(Would you like) anything else?

Yes, I'd also like…

Wǒ hái yào...
我还要…

No, thank you. That's all

Búyào le, xièxie
不要了, 谢谢

Could you show me…?

Qǐng ná...gěi wǒ kànkan
请拿…给我看看

I'd prefer…

Wǒ xǐhuan...
我喜欢…

This is not what I'm looking for

Zhè búshì wǒ yào de
这不是我要的

Thank you, I'll keep looking

Méiguānxi, wǒ zài kànkan
没关系, 我再看看

Do you have something…?

Yǒu méiyǒu...?
有没有…?

– less expensive?

piányi (yì) diǎnr de?
便宜(一)点儿的?

– smaller?

xiǎo (yì) diǎnr de?
小(一)点儿的?

– larger?

dà (yì) diǎnr de?
大(一)点儿的?

Shopping

10

I'll take this one	**Wǒ jiù yào zhè ge** 我就要这个
Does it come with instructions?	**Yǒu méiyǒu shuōmíngshū** 有没有说明书
It's too expensive	**Tài guì le** 太贵了
I'll give you…	**Wǒ chū…kuàiqián, zěnmeyàng?** 我出…块钱，怎么样？
Could you keep this for me?	**Qǐng tì wǒ liúzhe zhè ge** 请替我留着这个
I'll come back for it later	**Wǒ yìhuǐr zài lái mǎi** 我一会儿再来买
Do you have a bag for me, please?	**Qǐng gěi wǒ yí ge dàizi** 请给我一个袋子
Could you gift wrap it, please?	**Qǐng gěi wǒ bāochéng lǐwù** 请给我包成礼物

对不起，我们没有这种 **Duìbuqǐ, wǒmen méiyǒu zhè zhǒng**	I'm sorry, we don't have that
对不起，都卖完了 **Duìbuqǐ, dōu mài wánliǎo**	I'm sorry, we're sold out
对不起，要等到…才有货 **Duìbuqǐ, yào děngdào…cái yǒu huò**	I'm sorry, it won't come in until…
请到付款台结账 **Qǐng dào fùkuǎntái jiézhàng**	Please pay at the cash register
我们不接受信用卡 **Wǒmen bù jiēshòu xìnyòngkǎ**	We don't accept credit cards
我们不接受旅行支票 **Wǒmen bù jiēshòu lǚxíng zhīpiào**	We don't accept traveler's checks

10.2 Food

I'd like half a kilo/five hundred grams of…	**Wǒ yào bàn gōngjīn/wǔbǎi kè…** 我要半公斤／五百克…

I'd like a kilo of… **Wǒ yào yī gōngjīn…**
我要一公斤…

Could you cut it up for me, please? **Qǐng bāng wǒ qiēkāi**
请帮我切开

Can I order it? **Wǒ kěyǐ dìnggòu ma?**
我可以订购吗?

I'll pick it up tomorrow at… **Wǒ míngtiān...lái qǔ**
我明天…来取

Can you eat/drink this? **Zhè ge kěyǐ chī/hē ma?**
这个可以吃／喝吗?

What's in it? **Lǐmiàn yǒu shénme?**
里面有什么?

10.3 Clothing and shoes

I'd like something to go with this **Yǒu méiyǒu shénme pèi zhè ge de?**
有没有什么配这个的?

Do you have shoes to match this? **Yǒu méiyǒu pèi zhè ge de xié?**
有没有配这个的鞋?

I'm a size…in the U.S. **Wǒ chuān (Měiguó)...hào de**
我穿(美国)…号的

Can I try this on? **Wǒ kěyǐ shìchuān ma?**
我可以试穿吗?

Where's the fitting room? **Shìyīshì zài nǎlǐ?**
试衣室在哪里?

It doesn't suit me **Zhè (jiàn) bù hé wǒ chuān**
这(件)不合我穿

This is the right size **Zhège dàxiǎo zhènghǎo**
这个大小正好

It doesn't look good on me **Wǒ chuānqǐlái bù hǎokàn**
我穿起来不好看

Do you have these in…? **Zhèxiē yǒu méiyǒu...de?**
这些有没有…的?

– white	**báisè** 白色
– black	**hēisè** 黑色
– green	**lǜsè** 绿色
– red	**hóngsè** 红色
– blue	**lánsè** 蓝色
– yellow	**huángsè** 黄色
The heel's too high/low	**Xiégēn tài gāo/ǎi le** 鞋跟太高／矮了
Is this real leather?	**Zhè shì zhēn pí ma?** 这是真皮吗?
Is this genuine hide?	**Zhè shì zhēn shòupí ma?** 这是真兽皮吗?
I'm looking for a…for a…year-old child	**Wǒ zhǎo yí (ge)…sòng gěi…suì xiǎohái** 我找一（个）…送给…岁小孩
I'd like a…	**Wǒ yào yí jiàn…** 我要一件…
– silk	**zhēnsī de** 真丝的
– cotton	**miánbù de** 棉布的
– woolen	**máoliào de** 毛料的
– linen	**yàmábù de** 亚麻布的
At what temperature should I wash it?	**Wǒ yīnggāi yòng shénme shuǐwēn xǐ?** 我应该用什么水温洗?
Will it shrink in the wash?	**Huì suōshuǐ ma?** 会缩水吗?

手洗	勿用甩干机干燥	勿用熨斗熨
shǒuxǐ	**wù yòng shuǎigànjī gānzào**	**wù yòng yùndǒu yùn**
Hand wash	Do not spin dry	Do not iron
干洗	平放	可用洗衣机洗
gānxǐ	**píng fàng**	**kěyòng xǐyījī xǐ**
Dry clean	Lay flat	Machine washable

At the cobbler

Could you mend these shoes?	**Zhè shuāng xié kěyǐ xiūbǔ ma?** 这双鞋可以修补吗？
Could you resole these shoes?	**Qǐng gěi zhè shuāng xié huàn dǐ** 请给这双鞋换底
When will they be ready?	**Shénme shíhou néng qǔ?** 什么时候能取？
I'd like…, please	**Qǐng gěi wǒ...** 请给我…
– a can of shoe polish	**yì hé xiéyóu** 一盒鞋油
– a pair of shoelaces	**yì shuāng xiédài** 一双鞋带

(10.4) At the hairdresser

Do I have to make an appointment?	**Wǒ yào yùyuē ma?** 我要预约吗？
Can I come in right now?	**Wǒ kěyǐ xiànzài lái ma?** 我可以现在来吗？
How long will I have to wait?	**Yào děng duōjiǔ?** 要等多久？
I'd like a shampoo/ haircut	**Wǒ xiǎng xǐtóu/lǐfà** 我想洗头／理发
I'd like a shampoo for oily/dry hair, please	**Wǒ xiǎng xǐtóu. Wǒ de tóufa bǐjiào yóu/gān** 我想洗头。我的头发比较油／干

I'd like an anti-dandruff shampoo	**Wǒ yào qù tóupí de xǐfàjì** 我要去头皮的洗发剂
I'd like a color-rinse shampoo, please	**Wǒ yào bǎosè de xǐfàjì** 我要保色的洗发剂
I'd like a shampoo with conditioner, please	**Wǒ yào dài èrhéyī de xǐfàjì** 我要带二合一的洗发剂
I'd like highlights, please	**Qǐng gěi wǒ jiādiǎn xiǎnyǎn de yánsè** 请给我加点显眼的颜色
Do you have a color chart, please?	**Yǒu méiyǒu sèpǔ?** 有没有色谱？
I'd like to keep the same color	**Wǒ xiǎng bǎochí tóngyàng de yánsè** 我想保持同样的颜色
I'd like it darker/lighter	**Wǒ yào sè shēn/qiǎn yìdiǎn** 我要色深／浅一点
I'd like/don't want hairspray	**Qǐng gěi wǒ/búyào gěi wǒ pēn dìngxíngjiāo** 请给我／不要给我喷定型胶
– gel	**fàlà** 发蜡
– lotion	**xǐfàlù/yíngyǎngjì** 洗发露／营养剂
I'd like short bangs	**Wǒ yào duǎn yìdiǎn de liúhǎir** 我要短一点的刘海儿
Not too short at the back	**Hòumiàn de tóufà qǐng búyào jiǎnde tài duǎn** 后面的头发请不要剪得太短
Not too long	**Búyào tài cháng** 不要太长
I'd like it curly	**Wǒ yào tàng juǎnfà** 我要烫卷发
I don't like it too curly	**Wǒ búyào tàng de tài juǎn** 我不要烫得太卷
It needs a little/a lot taken off	**Wǒ xūyào xuēbáo yìdiǎn/hěnduō** 我需要削薄一点／很多

I like a completely different style/ a different cut	**Wǒ yào jiǎn yí ge wánquán bùtóng de fàxíng** 我要剪一个完全不同的发型
I'd like it the same as in this photo	**Wǒ yào jiǎn xiàng zhè zhāng zhàopiàn yíyàng de fàxíng** 我要剪像这张照片一样的发型
– as that woman's	**Wǒ yào jiǎn xiàng zhè wèi nǚshì yíyàng de fàxíng** 我要剪像这位女士一样的发型
Could you turn the drier up/down a bit?	**Qǐng bǎ chuīfēngjī tiáogāo/tiáodī yìdiǎn** 请把吹风机调高／调低一点
I'd like a facial	**Wǒ xiǎng zuò yí ge miànmò** 我想做一个面膜
– a manicure	**Wǒ xiǎng xiū zhǐjiǎ** 我想修指甲
Could you trim my..., please?	**Qǐng gěi wǒ xiū yíxià...** 请给我修一下…
– bangs	**liúhǎir** 刘海儿
– beard/moustache	**húxū/xiǎohúzi** 胡须／小胡子
I'd like a shave, please	**Qǐng gěi wǒ guāgua húzi** 请给我刮刮胡子

你想剪什么发型？ **Nǐ xiǎng jiǎn shénme fàxíng?**	What style did you have in mind?
你想染成什么颜色？ **Nǐ xiǎng rǎn chéng shénme yánsè?**	What color did you want it?
温度合适吗？ **Wēndù héshì ma?**	Is the temperature all right for you?
你想看什么杂志吗？ **Nǐ xiǎng kàn shénme zázhì ma?**	Would you like something to read?
你想喝点饮料吗？ **Nǐ xiǎng hē diǎn yǐnliào ma?**	Would you like a drink?

11 Tourist Activities

11.1	Sightseeing	139
11.2	Places of interest	142
11.3	Going out	144
11.4	Nightlife	146
11.5	Cultural performances	146
11.6	Booking tickets	148

11. Tourist Activities

● **China National Tourist Office** (CNTA) is a government organization that promotes and looks after the tourism industry of China. It has 15 international overseas offices, including those in U.S., Canada, Australia and Asia. Its website (www.cnta.org.) provides lots of information for tourists going to China.

One can also get information on China's tourist spots, accommodations, etc from the Internet. Alternatively on arrival, pick up the relevant brochures from the Airport Information Desk or the local hotel information desk.

Most travelers arrive with a pre-arranged package from overseas agencies which are generally affiliated with two semi-government travel agencies in China—China International Travel Service, and China Travel Service. Both have branches in major cities and towns. In addition there are private travel agents such as the China Youth Travel Service which cater to individual travelers. All travel agencies mainly advise on tours and package deals with the flexibility of car hire (with driver) and personal guides. These offices are generally open every day.

11.1 Sightseeing

Places to Visit

● **Beijing,** as China's capital city, is the second largest city. It is the center of commerce and trade on Mainland China. The top places to visit in Beijing are:

- The **Palace Museum** (故宫 **Gùgōng**). The palace was built between 1406 and 1420, but was burnt down, rebuilt, and renovated several times. Admission is 60 RMB. Open from 08:30–17:30.

- The **Temple of Heaven** (天坛 **Tiāntán**). It was initially built in 1420, covering an area of 273 hectares. In 1998, it was included in the "List of World Heritages" by UNESCO; admission is 15 RMB, open from 06:00–22:30.

- The **Summer Palace** (颐和园 **Yíhéyuán**); admission is 30 RMB. Opens from 06:30–18:00.

- **Beijing National Stadium**, also known as the Bird's Nest (鸟巢 **Niǎocháo**), designed for use throughout the 2008 Summer Olympics and Paralympics. Now a tourist spot, it opens from 09:00–18:00 March to October; 09:00–17:00 November to February.

● **Shanghai** has lots to offer both first-timers and repeat visitors—from museums, cinemas, and arts to fashion. The famous places to visit in Shanghai are:

- The **Shanghai Museum** (上海博物馆 **Shànghǎi Bówùguǎn**), a museum of ancient Chinese art, situated on the People's Square (人民广场 **Rénmín Guǎngchǎng**); open to the public 09:00–17:00.

- **Shanghai World Financial Center** (上海环球金融中心 **Shànghǎi Huánqiú Jīnróng Zhōngxīn**), consisting of offices, hotels, conference rooms, observation desks and shopping malls on the ground floors; open daily 08:00–23:00.

- The **Oriental Pearl TV Tower** (东方明珠 **Dōngfāng Míngzhū**). It's one of the most famous landmarks in Shanghai.

● **Hong Kong**, a British colony until 1997, is known for its expansive skyline and deep natural harbor and is one of the most densely populated areas in the world. The places to visit are:

- **Avenue of Stars** (星光大道 **Xīngguāng Dàdào**), where you can see stunning views of the harbor tower above you, while the names of Hong Kong's movie icons lie beneath your feet.

- **The Peak** (太平山 **Tàipíngshān**); the mountain is located in the western half of Hong Kong Island where you can see the Victoria Harbor and the vibrant view of the city. It is open from 07:00–24:00.

- **Shopping areas and malls**. Hong Kong is known as the shopping paradise of Asia. You can find many shops and malls at every turn of the streets.

More information about the top attractions in China can be found from the website: http://en.cnta.gov.cn/TravelInChina/Forms/TravelInChina/Chinainbrief.shtml

故宫
Gùgōng
Palace Museum

紫禁城
Zǐjīnchéng
Forbidden City

天安门广场
Tiān'ānmén Guǎngchǎng
Tian'anmen Square

天坛
Tiāntán
Temple of Heaven

颐和园
Yíhéyuán
Summer Palace

八达岭（长城）
Bādálǐng (Chángchéng)
Badaling (Great Wall)

外滩
Wàitān
The Bund

豫园
Yùyuán
Yuyuan Garden

上海博物馆
Shànghǎi Bówùguǎn
Shanghai Museum

东方明珠
Dōngfāng Míngzhū
Oriental Pearl Tower

黄浦江
Huángpǔjiāng
Huangpu River

寒山寺
Hánshānsì
Hanshan Temple

兵马俑
Bīngmǎyǒng
Terracotta Army

黄河
Huánghé
Yellow River

九寨沟
Jiǔzhàigōu
Jiuzhaigou Valley

星光大道
Xīngguāng Dàdào
Avenue of Stars

太平山顶
Tàipíngshāndǐng
The Peak

女人街
Nǚrénjiē
Ladies' Market

11.2 Places of interest

Where's the Tourist Information, please?	**Qǐngwèn, lǚyóu zīxúntái zài nǎli?** 请问，旅游资询台在哪里？
Do you have a city map?	**Yǒu běnshì dìtú ma?** 有本市地图吗？
Where is the museum?	**Bówùguǎn zài nǎli?** 博物馆在哪里？
Where can I find a church?	**Nǎlǐ yǒu jiàotáng?** 哪里有教堂？
Could you give me some information about…?	**Nǐ kěyǐ gěi wǒ yǒuguān…de zīliào ma?** 你可以给我有关…的资料吗？
How much is this?	**Zhè ge duōshao qián?** 这个多少钱？

What are the main places of interest?	**Zhǔyào yóuwán de dìfāng yǒu nǎxiē?** 主要游玩的地方有哪些？
Could you point them out on the map?	**Qǐng zài dìtú shàng zhǐ gěi wǒ kànkan** 请在地图上指给我看看
What do you recommend?	**Nǐ tuījiàn nǎ ge jǐngdiǎn?** 你推荐哪个景点？
We'll be here for a few hours	**Wǒmen yào zài zhèlǐ dāi jǐ ge xiǎoshí/zhōngtóu** 我们要在这里呆几个小时／钟头
We'll be here for a day	**Wǒmen yào zài zhèlǐ dāi yìtiān** 我们要在这里呆一天
We'll be here for a week	**Wǒmen yào zài zhèlǐ dāi yí ge xīngqī** 我们要在这里呆一个星期
We're interested in…	**Wǒmen duì...gǎn xìngqù** 我们对⋯感兴趣
How long does it take?	**Yào zǒu duōjiǔ?** 要走多久？
Where does it start/ end?	**Zài nǎli kāishǐ/jiéshù?** 在哪里开始／结束？
Are there any boat trips?	**Yǒu méiyǒu zuòchuán de lǚyóu hángxiàn?** 有没有坐船的旅游航线？
Where can we board?	**Zài nǎli shàngchuán?** 在哪里上船？
Are there any bus tours?	**Yǒu méiyǒu zuò lǚyóuchē de lùxiàn?** 有没有坐旅游车的路线？
Where do we get on?	**Zài nǎli shàngchē?** 在哪里上车？
Is there a guide who speaks English?	**Yǒu méiyǒu dǎoyóu huì shuō Yīngyǔ de?** 有没有导游会说英语的？
What trips can we take around the area?	**Fùjìn yǒu shénme jǐngdiǎn zhídé qù wán de?** 附近有什么景点值得去玩的？

Are there any excursions?	**Yǒu méiyǒu duǎntú lǚyóu lùxiàn?** 有没有短途旅游路线?
Where do they go?	**Zhèxiē duǎntú lǚyóu qù nǎli?** 这些短途旅游去哪里?
How long is the excursion?	**Zhè ge duǎntú lǚyóu yǒu duō yuǎn?** 这个短途旅游有多远?
We'd like to go to…	**Wǒmen xiǎng qù…** 我们想去…
– the Palace Museum	**Gùgōng** 故宫
– the Forbidden City	**Zǐjīnchéng** 紫禁城
– Shanghai Museum	**Shànghǎi bówùguǎn** 上海博物馆
How much does it cost to…?	**Dào…duōshao qián?** 到…多少钱?
How much is the admission ticket?	**Ménpiào duōshao qián?** 门票多少钱?
How long do we stay in…?	**Wǒmen zài…dāi duōjiǔ?** 我们在…呆多久?
Are there any guided tours?	**Zhèxiē lǚyóutuán yǒu méiyǒu dǎoyóu?** 这些旅游团有没有导游?
Do you have English tour service?	**Yǒu méiyǒu Yīngyǔ jiǎngjiě fúwù?** 有没有英语讲解服务?
How much free time will we have there?	**Dàole nàli, wǒmen yǒu duōshao zìyóu huódòng shíjiān?** 到了那里, 我们有多少自由活动时间?
We want to have a walk around	**Wǒmen xiǎng zài fùjìn zǒuzou** 我们想在附近走走
Can we hire a guide?	**Kěyǐ gùyòng yí ge dǎoyóu ma?** 可以雇用一个导游吗?
What time does… open/close?	**…jǐdiǎn kāimén/guānmén?** …几点开门 / 关门?

What days are… open/closed?	**…nǎ tiān kāimén/guānmén?** ⋯哪天开门 / 关门？
What's the admission price?	**Rùchǎngfèi shì duōshǎo?** 入场费是多少？
Is there a group discount?	**Tuántǐ yǒu méiyǒu yōuhuì?** 团体有没有优惠？
Is there a child discount?	**Xiǎohái yǒu méiyǒu yōuhuì?** 小孩有没有优惠？
Is there a discount for senior citizens?	**Lǎorén yǒu méiyǒu yōuhuì?** 老人有没有优惠？
Can I take (flash) photos here?	**Zhèlǐ kěyǐ yòng shǎnguāngdēng zhàoxiàng ma?** 这里可以用闪光灯照相吗？
Can I film here?	**Zhèlǐ kěyǐ pāi lùxiàng ma?** 这里可以拍录像吗？
Do you have the brochure for…?	**Yǒu méiyǒu…xiǎocèzi?** 有没有⋯的小册子？
Do you have an English…?	**Yǒu méiyǒu Yīngwén de…** 有没有英文的⋯
– catalog?	**mùlù?** 目录？
– program?	**jiémùbiǎo?** 节目表？
– brochure?	**lǚyóushǒucè?** 旅游手册？

11.3 Going out

● **China** has an increasing number of bars, discos, late-night restaurants and coffee shops. In major cities there are various evening performances every night. Try to get in to see a martial arts or acrobatic performance, a concert or Beijing opera.

| Do you have this week's/ month's entertainment guide? | **Yǒu méiyǒu běnzhōu/běnyuè de yúlè zhǐ'nán?** 有没有本周 / 本月的娱乐指南？ |

What's on tonight?	**Jīnwǎn yǒu shénme hǎo jiémù?** 今晚有什么好节目？
We want to go to...	**Wǒmen xiǎng qù...** 我们想去…
What's playing at the cinema?	**Diànyǐngyuàn shàngyìng shénme?** 电影院上映什么？
What sort of film is that?	**Nà shì shénme diànyǐng?** 那是什么电影？
– suitable for everyone	**dàrén xiǎohái dōu néng kàn** 大人小孩都能看
– not suitable for people under 16	**shíliù suì yǐxià de értóng bùyí kàn** 十六岁以下的儿童不宜看
– subtitled	**yǒu zìmù de** 有字幕的
– dubbed	**fānyì pèiyīn de** 翻译配音的
What's on at...?	**...yǒu shénme shàngyìng?** …有什么上映？
– the theater?	**xìjù** 戏剧
– the opera?	**gējù** 歌剧
What's happening in the concert hall?	**Yīnyuètīng yǒu shénme biǎoyǎn?** 音乐厅有什么表演？
Where can I find a good nightclub around here?	**Fùjìn nǎli yǒu hǎo de yèzǒnghuì?** 附近哪里有好的夜总会？
Is it evening wear only?	**Yào chuān wǎnzhuāng ma?** 要穿晚装吗？
Should I/we dress up?	**Wǒ(men) yào chuānde zhèngshì ma?** 我（们）要穿得正式吗？
What time does the show start?	**Biǎoyǎn shénme shíhou kāiyǎn?** 表演什么时候开演？
Could you reserve some tickets for us?	**Qǐng gěi wǒmen yùdìng jǐ zhāng piào** 请给我们预订几张票

| We'd like to book…
seats/a table for… | **Wǒmen xiǎng dìng…ge rén de zuòr/
…gerén de zhuōzi**
我们想订…个人的座儿／个人的桌子 |

11.4 Nightlife

Where's the bar?	**Jiǔbā zài nǎli?** 酒吧在哪里？
Is there a disco here?	**Zhèlǐ yǒu dísīkē ma?** 这里有迪斯科吗？
Please bring me a beer	**Qǐng gěi wǒ lái yì bēi píjiǔ** 请给我来一杯啤酒
I'd like a glass of whisky	**Wǒ xiǎng yào yì bēi wēishìjì** 我想要一杯威士忌
straight	**bù jiā bīngkuài** 不加冰块
on the rocks	**jiā bīngkuài** 加冰块

11.5 Cultural performances

Activities

| Is there a…near by? | **Zhè fùjìn nǎlǐ yǒu…?**
这附近哪里有…？ |

茶楼 **chálóu** tea house	剧院 **jùyuàn** theater	京剧 **Jīngjù** Beijing Opera
音乐会 **yīnyuèhuì** concert	电影院 **diànyǐngyuàn** cinema	川剧变脸 **Chuānjùbiànliǎn** face-changing in Sichuan opera
杂技团 **zájìtuán** acrobatics troupe	博物馆 **bówùguǎn** museum	

传统市集
chuántǒng shìjí
traditional market

夜市
yèshì
night market

画廊
huàláng
gallery

港式点心
gǎngshì diǎnxīn
dim sum

麻辣火锅
málà huǒguō
spicy hotpot

夜景
yèjǐng
night view

– cinema

diànyǐngyuàn
电影院

– tea house

chálóu
茶楼

When does the…open
and close?

…jǐdiǎn kāimén, jǐdiǎn guānmén?
…几点开门，几点关门？

– gallery

huàláng
画廊

– museum

bówùguǎn
博物馆

Where can I see…?

Nǎlǐ kéyǐ kàn…?
哪里可以看…？

Where can I eat…?

Nǎlǐ kéyǐ chī…?
哪里可以吃…？

I'd like to see…

Wǒ xiǎng kàn…
我想看…

– Beijing Opera

Jīngjù
京剧

– local opera

dìfāngxì
地方戏

– face-changing in
Sichuan opera

Chuānjùbiànliǎn
川剧变脸

– an acrobatic
performance

zájì biǎoyǎn
杂技表演

– a song and dance show

gēwǔ
歌舞

– a martial arts
performance

wǔshù biǎoyǎn
武术表演

– folk dances   **mínjiān wǔdǎo**
民间舞蹈

– a Chinese classical   **guóyuè yǎnzòu**
  music concert   国乐演奏

– a Chinese movie   **Zhōngguó diànyǐng**
中国电影

– a kungfu/action movie   **wǔshùpiàn/dòngzuòpiàn**
武术片 / 动作片

I'd like to go to a concert **Wǒ xiǎng qù tīng yīnyuèhuì**
我想去听音乐会

I'd like to go to a   **Wǒ xiǎng qù tīng gēchànghuì**
  singing recital   我想去听歌唱会

Are there English   **Yǒu méiyǒu Yīngwén zìmù?**
  subtitles?   有没有英文字幕？

Are there any tickets for **Yǒu méiyǒu jīnwǎn de piào?**
  tonight's show?   有没有今晚的票？

How much are the least **Zuì piányi de zuòwèi duōshao qián?**
  expensive seats?   最便宜的座位多少钱？

How much are front   **Qiánpái zuòwèi duōshao qián?**
  row seats?   前排座位多少钱？

11.6 Booking tickets

...front row seats/a table **qiánpái de zuòr/zài qiánmiàn de...ge**
  for...at the front   **rén de zhuōzi**
前排的座儿 / 在前面的…个人的桌子

...seats in the middle/   **zhōngjiān de zuòr/zhōngjiān de zhuōzi**
  a table in the middle 中间的座儿 / 中间的桌子

...back row seats/a table **hòumiàn de zuòr/hòumiàn de zhuōzi**
  at the back   后面的座儿 / 后面的桌子

Could I reserve...seats   **Wǒ xiǎng yùdìng...zhāng...diǎn**
  for the...o'clock   **kāiyǎn de piào**
  performance?   我想预订…张…点开演的票

Are there any seats left for tonight?	**Hái yǒu méiyǒu jīnwǎn de piào?** 还有没有今晚的票?
How much is a ticket?	**Duōshǎo qián yì zhāng piào?** 多少钱一张票?
When can I pick up the tickets?	**Piào shénme shíhou néng qǔ?** 票什么时候能取?
I've got a reservation	**Wǒ yùdìngle piào** 我预订了票
My name's...	**Wǒde míngzi jiào...** 我的名字叫…

你想预订哪一场的票? **Nǐ xiǎng yùdìng nǎ yìchǎng de piào?**	Which performance do you want to reserve for?
你想坐在哪里? **Nǐ xiǎng zuò zài nǎli?**	Where would you like to sit?
票都卖完了 **Piào dōu mài wánle**	Everything's sold out
只有站的位子 **Zhǐyǒu zhàn de wèizi**	It's standing room only
我们只有楼厅的票了 **Wǒmen zhǐyǒu lóutīng de piàole**	We've only got circle seats left
我们只有上层楼厅的票了 **Wǒmen zhǐyǒu shàngcéng lóutīng de piàole**	We've only got upper circle (way upstairs) seats left
我们只有前排的票了 **Wǒmen zhǐyǒu qiánpái de piàole**	We've only got front row seats left
我们只有后排的票了 **Wǒmen zhǐyǒu hòupái de piàole**	We've only got seats left at the back
你要几张票? **Nǐ yào jǐzhāng piào?**	How many seats would you like?
你要在…点以前来取票 **Nǐ yào zài...diǎn yǐqián lái qǔ piào**	You'll have to pick up the tickets before... o'clock
这是你的位子 **Zhè shì nǐ de wèizi**	This is your seat
(对不起), 你坐错位子了 **(Duìbuqǐ), nǐ zuòcuò wèizile**	You are in the wrong seat

149

12 Sports Activities

12.1 Sporting questions   151

12.2 By the waterfront   151

12.3 In the snow   153

12. Sports Activities

12.1 Sporting questions

Where's the stadium/ gymnasium?	**Yùndòngchǎng/Tǐyùguǎn zài nǎli?** 运动场 / 体育馆在哪里?
Can we go to see a… game?	**Wǒmen kěyǐ qù kàn…bǐsài ma?** 我们可以去看…比赛吗?
– soccer	**zúqiú** 足球
– basketball	**lánqiú** 篮球
– badminton	**yǔmáoqiú** 羽毛球
– table tennis	**pīngpāng qiú** 乒乓球
When does the game begin?	**Bǐsài shénme shíhou kāishǐ?** 比赛什么时候开始?
What's the score?	**Bǐfēn shì duōshao?** 比分是多少?
I've won	**Wǒ yíng le** 我赢了
I've lost	**Wǒ shū le** 我输了
We're even	**Dǎchéng píngshǒu** 打成平手

12.2 By the waterfront

Is it far (to walk) to the sea?	**Zhèlǐ qù hǎibiān yuǎn ma?** 这里去海边远吗?
Is there a…around here?	**Zhèlǐ yǒu méiyǒu…?** 这里有没有…?

– swimming pool	**yóuyǒngchí** 游泳池
– sandy beach	**shātān/hǎitān** 沙滩 / 海滩
Are there any rocks here?	**Zhèlǐ yǒu méiyǒu shítou?** 这里有没有石头？
When's high/low tide?	**Shénme shíhou cháozhǎng/cháo tuì?** 什么时候潮涨 / 潮退？
What's the water temperature?	**Shuǐwēn shì duōshao?** 水温是多少？
Is it deep here?	**Shuǐ shēn bu shēn?** 水深不深？
Is it safe (for children) to swim here?	**(Xiǎohái) zài zhèlǐ yóuyǒng ānquán ma?** （小孩）在这里游泳安全吗？
Are there any…?	**Zhèlǐ yǒu méiyǒu…?** 这里有没有 … ？
– currents	**jíliú** 急流
– sharks	**shāyú** 鲨鱼
– jellyfish	**shuǐmǔ** 水母
What does that flag mean?	**Nà miàn qí shì shénme yìsi?** 那面旗是什么意思？
What does that buoy mean?	**Nà ge fúbiāo shì shénme yìsi?** 那个浮标是什么意思？
Is there a lifeguard on duty?	**Zhèlǐ yǒu méiyǒu jiùshēngyuán zhíbān?** 这里有没有救生员值班？
Where can I get…?	**Nǎli yǒu…?** 哪里有 … ？
– a bathing suit	**yóuyǒng yī** 游泳衣

– a chair	**yǐzi** 椅子
– a beach umbrella	**tàiyáng sǎn** 太阳伞
– a towel	**máojīn** 毛巾
Where can I have a shower?	**Nǎli kěyǐ línyù?** 哪里可以淋浴？

危险 **wéixiǎn** Danger	这里不准游泳／钓鱼 **zhèlǐ bùzhǔn yóuyǒng/diàoyú** No swimming/fishing here

---

 In the snow

Can I take ski lessons here?	**Zhèlǐ yǒu méiyǒu xué huáxuě de bān?** 这里有没有学滑雪的班？
For beginners/ intermediates	**Chūjíbān/zhōngjíbān** 初级班／中级班
How large are the groups?	**Yìbān yǒu duōshao rén?** 一班有多少人？
What languages are the classes in?	**Shàngkè jiǎng shénme yǔyán?** 上课讲什么语言？
I'd like a lift pass, please	**Qǐng gěi wǒ diàolánpiào** 请给我吊篮票
Where are the beginners' slopes?	**Chūjí huáxuědào zài nǎli?** 初级滑雪道在哪里？
Where are the intermediate runs?	**Zhōngjí huáxuědào zài nǎli?** 中级滑雪道在哪里？
Are there any cross-country ski runs around here?	**Zhèlǐ yǒu méiyǒu yuèyě huáxuědào?** 这里有没有越野滑雪道？
Have the cross-country runs been marked?	**Yuèyě huáxuědào yǒu méiyǒu biāozhì?** 越野滑雪道有没有标志？

Are the...open?	**...kāi bu kāi?**
	…开不开?
– the ski lifts	**huáxuě diàolán**
	滑雪吊篮
– the chair lifts	**shàngshān diàochē**
	上山吊车
– the runs	**huáxuědào**
	滑雪道
– the cross-country runs	**yuèyě huáxuědào**
	越野滑雪道

13 Health Matters

13.1	Calling a doctor	156
13.2	What's wrong?	157
13.3	The consultation	158
13.4	Medications and prescriptions	163
13.5	At the dentist	164

13. Health Matters

● **If you become ill** or need emergency treatment, you can call 120 or 999 for emergency treatment. There are special departments for foreign nationals in many large hospitals where they have better facilities and you are expected to pay more for the treatment. Alternatively, foreign nationals can choose to go to the Casualty department at the nearest hospital. The procedures are: first, go directly to Casualty to register; second, have your illness treated; and third, settle the bill. Of course, in critical cases, treatment will come first and then registration and payment later.

13.1 Calling a doctor

Could you call (get) a doctor quickly, please?	**Qǐng gěi wǒ zhǎo ge dàifu/yīshēng** 请给我找个大夫／医生
When are the doctor's working hours?	**Dàifū/Yīshēng jǐdiǎn dào jǐdiǎn kànbìng?** 大夫／医生几点到几点看病？
When can the doctor come?	**Dàifū/Yīshēng shénme shíhou néng lái?** 大夫／医生什么时候能来？
Could I make an appointment to see the doctor?	**Wǒ xiǎng yùyuē kànbìng, kěyǐ ma?** 我想预约看病，可以吗？
I've got an appointment to see the doctor at... o'clock	**Wǒ gēn yùyuēhǎo...diǎnzhōng kànbìng** 我跟预约好⋯点钟看病
Which pharmacy is on night/weekend duty?	**Nǎ ge yàofáng wǎnshang/zhōumò yíngyè?** 哪个药房晚上／周末营业？

I don't feel well	**Wǒ bú tài shūfu** 我不太舒服
I'm dizzy	**Wǒ tóuyūn** 我头晕
I'm ill	**Wǒ bìng le** 我病了
I feel sick (nauseous)	**Wǒ xiǎng tǔ** 我想吐
I've got a cold	**Wǒ gǎnmào le** 我感冒了
I've got diarrhea	**Wǒ fùxiè/xiè dùzi le** 我腹泻／泻肚子了
I have trouble breathing	**Wǒ gǎnjué hūxī kùnnan** 我感觉呼吸困难
I feel tired all over	**Wǒ húnshēn méijìn** 我浑身没劲
I've burnt myself	**Wǒ shāoshāng le** 我烧伤了
It hurts here	**Zhèlǐ téng** 这里疼
I've been sick (vomited)	**Wǒ ǒutù le** 我呕吐了
I'm running a temperature of...degrees	**Wǒ fāshāo, ...dù** 我发烧, …度
I've been...	**Wǒ...** 我…
– stung by a wasp	**bèi huángfēng zhēle** 被黄蜂蛰了
– stung by an insect	**bèi shénme chóngzi zhēle** 被什么虫子蛰了
– stung by a jellyfish	**bèi shuǐmǔ zhēle** 被水母蛰了

– bitten by a dog	**bèi gǒu yǎole** 被狗咬了
– bitten by a snake	**bèi shé yǎole** 被蛇咬了
I've cut myself	**Wǒ gēshāng zìjǐ le** 我割伤自己了
I've burned myself	**Wǒ shāoshāng zìjǐ le** 我烧伤自己了
I've grazed/scratched myself	**Wǒ cāshāng/zhuāshāng zìjǐ le** 我擦伤／抓伤自己了
I've had a fall	**Wǒ diēshāng le** 我跌伤了

13.3 The consultation

你哪里不舒服？ **Nǐ nǎlǐ bú shūfú?**	What seems to be the problem?
你有这个病情多久了？ **Nǐ yǒu zhège bìngqíng duōjiǔle?**	How long have you had these complaints?
以前有过这个病吗？ **Yǐqián yǒuguò zhè ge bìng ma?**	Have you had this trouble before?
发烧吗？多少度？ **Fāshāo ma? Duōshao dù?**	Do you have a temperature? What is it?
请解开上衣 **Qǐng jiěkāi shàngyī**	Open your shirt, please
请脱下上衣 **Qǐng tuōxià shàngyī**	Strip to the waist, please
你可以在这里脱衣服 **Nǐ kěyǐ zài zhèlǐ tuō yīfú**	You can undress here
请卷起左／右袖子 **Qǐng juǎn qǐ zuǒ/yòu xiùzi**	Roll up your left/right sleeve, please
请躺在这里 **Qǐng tǎng zài zhèlǐ**	Lie down here, please

疼不疼? **Téng bù téng?**	Does this hurt?
深呼吸 **Shēnhūxī**	Breathe deeply
张开嘴 **Zhāngkāi zuǐ**	Open your mouth

I've sprained my ankle	**Wǒ niǔshāng le** 我扭伤了
Could I have a female doctor, please?	**Qǐng gěi wǒ zhǎo yí wèi nǚ dàifu/ yīshēng** 请给我找一位女大夫／医生
I'd like the morning-after pill	**Wǒ yàomǎi shìhòu bìyùnyào** 我要买事后避孕药

Patients' medical history

I'm a diabetic	**Wǒ yǒu tángniàobìng** 我有糖尿病
I have a heart condition	**Wǒ yǒu xīnzàngbìng** 我有心脏病
I'm asthmatic	**Wǒ huàn qìchuǎn bìng de** 我患气喘病的
I'm allergic to…	**Wǒ duì…guòmǐn de** 我对…过敏的
I'm…months pregnant	**Wǒ huáiyùn…ge yuè** 我怀孕…个月
I'm on a diet	**Wǒ zài jiéshí** 我在节食
I'm on medication/ the pill	**Wǒ zài fú yàowù/bìyùnyào** 我在服药物／避孕药
I've had a heart attack once before	**Wǒ céng yǒuguò yí cì xīnzàngbìng fāzuò** 我曾有过一次心脏病发作

I've had a(n)...operation **Wǒ yǐqián zuòguò...shǒushù**
我以前做过…手术

I've been ill recently **Wǒ zuìjìn bìngguo yí cì**
我最近病过一次

你对什么过敏？
Nǐ duì shénme guòmǐn?   Do you have any allergies?

你现在吃什么药？
Nǐ xiànzài chī shénme yào?   Are you on any medication?

你是不是在节食？
Nǐ shì bushì zài jiéshí ma?   Are you on a diet?

你怀孕了吗？
Nǐ huáiyùnle ma?   Are you pregnant?

你打过破伤风针吗？
Nǐ dǎguò pòshāngfēng zhēn ma?   Have you had a tetanus injection?

The diagnosis

不要紧   It's nothing serious
Búyàojǐn

你的…断了   Your...is broken
Nǐ de...duàn le

你扭伤了   You've got a sprained
Nǐ niǔshāng le

你的…扯破了   You've got a torn...
Nǐ de...chěpò le

你感染／发炎了   You've got an infection
Nǐ gǎnrǎn/fāyán le

你的…发炎了   You've got some inflammation
Nǐ de...fāyán le

你得了阑尾炎   You've got appendicitis
Nǐ dé le lánwěiyán

你得了气管炎   You've got bronchitis
Nǐ dé le qìguǎnyán

你得了性病
Nǐ dé le xìngbìng

You've got a venereal disease

你得了感冒
Nǐ dé le gǎnmào

You've got the flu

你的心脏病发作了
Nǐ de xīnzàngbìng fāzuò le

You've had a heart attack

你得了肺炎
Nǐ dé le fèiyán

You've got pneumonia

你得了胃炎 / 胃溃疡
Nǐ dé le wèiyán/wèikuìyáng

You've got gastritis/an ulcer

你扯伤了肌肉
Nǐ chěshāng le jīròu

You've pulled a muscle

你的阴道发炎了
Nǐde yīndào fāyán le

You've got a vaginal infection

你进食中毒了
Nǐ jìnshí zhòngdú le

You've got food poisoning

你中暑了
Nǐ zhòngshǔ le

You've got sunstroke

你对…过敏
Nǐ duì...guòmǐn

You're allergic to…

你怀孕了
Nǐ huáiyùn le

You're pregnant

我要给你化验你的血 / 尿 / 大便
Wǒ yào gěi nǐ huàyàn nǐde xuè/
niào/dàbiàn

I'd like to have your blood/urine/
stools tested

要缝合伤口
Yào fénghé shāngkǒu

It needs stitches

我把你交给专科医生
Wǒ bǎ nǐ jiāo gěi zhuānkē yīshēng

I'm referring you to a specialist

我把你送进医院
Wǒ bǎ nǐ sòng jìn yīyuàn

I'm sending you to the hospital

你要去做透视
Nǐ yào qù zuò tòushì

You'll need some x-rays taken

请你在候诊室等候
Qǐng nǐ zài hòuzhěnshì děnghòu

Could you wait in the waiting
room, please?

你需要做手术
Nǐ xūyào zuò shǒushù

You'll need an operation

I need something for
diarrhea

Wǒ yào zhì fùxiè de yào
我要治腹泻的药

I need something for a cold	**Wǒ yào zhì gǎnmào de yào** 我要治感冒的药
I've got a stomach ulcer	**Wǒ yǒu wèikuìyáng** 我有胃溃疡
I've got my period	**Wǒ yuèjīng gāng lái** 我月经刚来
Is it contagious?	**Huì chuánrǎn ma?** 会传染吗?
How long do I have to stay...?	**Wǒ yào zài...duōjiǔ?** 我要在…多久?
– in bed	**tǎng zài chuángshàng** 躺在床上
– in the hospital	**zhùyuàn** 住院
Do I have to go on a special diet?	**Wǒ yào tèbié jiéshí ma?** 我要特别节食吗?
Am I allowed to travel?	**Wǒ kěyǐ qù lǚyóu ma?** 我可以去旅游吗?
Can I make another appointment?	**Wǒ kěyǐ zài yùyuē ge shíjiān ma?** 我可以再预约个时间吗?
I'll come back tomorrow	**Wǒ míngtiān huílai** 我明天回来
How do I take this medicine?	**Zhè zhǒng yào zěnme chī?** 这种药怎么吃?

请明天／…天后回来复诊
Qǐng míngtiān/...tiān hòu huílái fùzhěn

Come back tomorrow/in...days' time

13.4 Medications and prescriptions

How many pills/drops/spoonfuls/tablets each time?	**Měi cì duōshao piàn/dī/sháo/lì?** 每次多少片 / 滴 / 勺 / 粒?
How many injections each time?	**Měi cì dǎ jǐ zhēn?** 每次打几针?
How many times a day?	**Yì tiān duōshao cì?** 一天多少次?
I've forgotten my medication	**Wǒ wàngle chī yào** 我忘了吃药
At home I take…	**Zài jiā wǒ chī…** 在家我吃…
Could you write a prescription for me, please?	**Qǐng gěi wǒ kāi ge yàofāng** 请给我开个药方

我给你开抗生素 / 咳嗽药水 / 镇静剂 / 止痛药 **Wǒ gěi nǐ kāi kàngshēngsù/késou yàoshuǐ/zhènjìngjì/zhǐtòng yào**	I'm prescribing antibiotics/ a cough mixture/a tranquilizer/painkillers
好好休息 **Hǎohǎo xiūxí**	Have lots of rest
不要外出 **Búyào wàichū**	Stay indoors
躺在床上 **Tǎng zài chuángshàng**	Stay in bed

药丸 **yàowán** pills	勺 / 茶勺 **sháo/cháshǎo** spoonful/teaspoonful	吞下 **tūn xià** swallow (whole)	揉搓 **róucuo** rub on
饭前 **fàn qián** before meals	每…钟头 / 小时 **měi…zhōngtóu/xiǎoshí** every…hours	外用 **wàiyòng** external use only	打针 **dǎzhēn** injections

饭后 **fàn hòu** after meals	全部吃完大夫／ 医生开的药 **quánbù chī wán dàifū/ yīshēng kāi de yào** finish the prescription	溶化在水里 **rónghuà zài shuǐlǐ** dissolve in water	药膏 **yàogāo** ointment
药片 **yàopiàn** tablets		吃／喝（药） **chī/hē (yào)** take	…天 **…tiān** for…days
滴剂 **dī jì** drops	这种药影响开车 **Zhè zhǒng yào yǐngxiǎng kāichē** this medication impairs your driving	每天…次 **měi tiān…cì** …times a day	

13.5 At the dentist

Do you know a good dentist?	**Zhèlǐ yǒu hǎo de yákē yīshēng ma?** 这里有好的牙科医生吗?
Could you make a dentist's appointment for me?	**Qǐng gěi wǒ yùyuē yákē yīshēng** 请给我预约牙科医生
It's urgent	**Zhè shì jǐnjí de** 这是紧急的
Can I come in today, please	**Wǒ néng jīntiān lái ma?** 我能今天来吗?
I have a (terrible) toothache	**Wǒde yá téngsǐ wǒ le** 我的牙疼死我了
Could you prescribe/ give me a painkiller?	**Kěyǐ gěi wǒ kāi ge zhǐtòngyào ma?** 可以给我开个止痛药吗?
I've got a broken tooth	**Wǒde yá zhuànghuàile** 我的牙撞坏了
My filling's come out	**Wǒ bǔyá de tiánchōngwù diàochūlai le** 我补牙的填充物掉出来了
I've got a broken crown	**Wǒ de chǐguān zhuànghuài le** 我的齿冠撞坏了
I'd like a local anaesthetic	**Qǐng gěi wǒ dǎ máyào** 请给我打麻药
I don't want a local anaesthetic	**Qǐng búyào gěi wǒ dǎ máyào** 请不要给我打麻药

I'm giving you a local anaesthetic	**Wǒ xiànzài gěi nǐ dǎ máyào** 我现在给你打麻药
Could you do a temporary repair?	**Kěyǐ gěi wǒ línshí bǔ yì bǔyá ma?** 可以给我临时补一补牙吗?
I don't want this tooth pulled	**Wǒ búyào bá zhè kē yá** 我不要拔这颗牙
My denture is broken	**Wǒ de jiǎyá zhuànghuài le** 我的假牙撞坏了

13

可以修理吗? **Kěyǐ xiūlǐ ma?**	Can you fix it?
你哪颗牙疼? **Nǐ nǎ kē yá téng?**	Which tooth hurts?
你的牙神经发炎 **Nǐ de yá shénjīng fāyán**	You've got an abscess
我得给你拔这颗牙 **Wǒ děi gěi nǐ bá zhè kē yá**	I'll have to pull this tooth
我得给你补／锉平这颗牙 **Wǒ děi gěi nǐ bǔ/cuò píng zhè kē yá**	I'll have to fill/file this tooth
我得钻这颗牙 **Wǒ děi zuān zhè kē yá**	I'll have to drill it
请张开你的嘴 **Qǐng zhāngkāi nǐde zuǐ**	Open wide, please
请张开得大一点 **Qǐng zhāngkāi de dà yìdiǎn**	Open wider, please
请把你的嘴合起来 **Qǐng bǎ nǐde zuǐ hé qǐlái**	Close your mouth, please
请咬紧你的牙 **Qǐng yǎojǐn nǐde yá**	Bite together, please
请漱口 **Qǐng shùkǒu**	Rinse, please
还疼吗? **Hái téng ma?**	Does it hurt still?

14 Emergencies

14.1 Asking for help   167

14.2 Lost items   168

14.3 Accidents   169

14.4 Theft   170

14.5 Missing person   170

14.6 The police   172

14. Emergencies

14.1 Asking for help

Help!
Jiùmìng a!
救命啊！

Get help quickly!
Kuài jiào rén lái bāngmáng!
快叫人来帮忙！

Fire!
Jiùhuǒ la!
救火啦！

Police!
Wǒ yào jǐngchá!
我要警察！

Get a doctor!
Qù zhǎo dàifū/yīshēng lái!
去找大夫／医生来！

Quick/Hurry!
Kuài!
快！

Danger!
Wēixiǎn!
危险！

Watch out!/ Be careful!
Dāngxīn!/Xiǎoxīn!
当心！／小心！

Stop!
Zhànzhù/Tíngzhù
站住／停住

Get your hands off me!
Nákāi nǐde shǒu
拿开你的手

Let go!
Fàngkāi wǒ!
放开我！

Stop thief!
Zhuā zéi la!
抓贼啦！

Could you help me, please?
Qǐng bāng ge máng, kěyǐ ma?
请帮个忙，可以吗？

Where's the police station/emergency exit/fire escape?
Gōng'ānjú (Jǐngchájú)/jǐnjí chūkǒu/ tàipíngtī zài nǎli?
公安局（警察局）／紧急出口／太平梯 在哪里？

Where's the nearest fire extinguisher?	**Zuìjìnde mièhuǒqì zài nǎli?** 最近的灭火器在哪里？
Call the fire department!	**Kuài jiào xiāofángjú!** 快叫消防局！
Call the police!	**Kuài jiào jǐngchá!** 快叫警察！
Call an ambulance!	**Kuài jiào jiùhùchē!** 快叫救护车！
Where's the nearest phone?	**Zuìjìnde diànhuà zài nǎlǐ?** 最近的电话在哪里？
Could I use your phone?	**Kěyǐ jièyòng nǐde diànhuà ma?** 可以借用你的电话吗？
What's the emergency number?	**Jǐnjí hàomǎ shì shénme?** 紧急号码是什么？
What's the number for the police?	**Gōng'ānjú/jǐngchájú de diànhuà shì shénme?** 公安局／警察局的电话是什么？

14.2 Lost items

I've lost my wallet/purse	**Wǒ diūshīle qiánbāo** 我丢失了钱包
I lost my…here yesterday	**Wǒ zuótiān zài zhèlǐ diūle wǒde...** 我昨天在这里丢了我的…
I left my…here	**Wǒ zài zhèlǐ diūxià wǒde...** 我在这里丢下我的…
Did you find my…?	**Nǐ zhǎodào wǒde...le ma?** 你找到我的…了吗？
It was right here	**Wǒ jìde shì fàng zài zhèlǐ de** 我记得是放在这里的
It's very valuable	**Zhè shì hěn guìzhòng de** 这是很贵重的
Where's the lost and found office?	**Shīwù zhāolǐngchù zài nǎli?** 失物招领处在哪里？

14.3 Accidents

There's been an accident	**(Wǒmen) zhèr chū shìgù le** （我们）这儿出事故了
Someone's fallen into the water	**Yǒurén diàojìn shuǐlǐ le!** 有人掉进水里了！
There's a fire	**Shīhuǒ le!/Zháohuǒ le!** 失火了！／着火了！
Is anyone hurt?	**Yǒu méiyǒu rén shòushāng?** 有没有人受伤？
Nobody/someone has been injured	**Méi rén shòushāng/Yǒu rén shòushāng le** 没人受伤／有人受伤了
Someone's still trapped inside the car	**Yǒu rén hái kùn zài chē lǐmiàn** 有人还困在车里面
It's not too bad	**Hái suàn hǎo** 还算好
Don't worry	**Búyào dānxīn** 不要担心
Leave everything the way it is, please	**Qǐng ràng suǒyǒu de dōngxi bǎochí yuánzhuàng** 请让所有的东西保持原状
I want to talk to the police first	**Wǒ yào xiān gēn jǐngchá tántan** 我要先跟警察谈谈
I want to take a photo first	**Wǒ yào xiān pāi ge zhào** 我要先拍个照
Here's my name and address	**Zhè shì wǒde míngzì hé dìzhǐ** 这是我的名字和地址
May I have your name and address?	**Qǐng gěi wǒ nǐde míngzì hé dìzhǐ** 请给我你的名字和地址
Could I see your identity card/your insurance papers?	**Qǐng gěi wǒ kànkan nǐde shēnfènzhèng/bǎoxiǎndān** 请给我看看你的身份证／保险单
Will you act as a witness?	**Nǐ yuànyì zuò zhèng ma?** 你愿意作证吗？

I need this information for insurance purposes	**Wǒde bǎoxiǎn gōngsī xūyào zhèxiē zīliào** 我的保险公司需要这些资料
Are you insured?	**Nǐ yǒu bǎoxiǎn ma?** 你有保险吗？
Third party or all inclusive?	**Nǐ mǎi de bǎoxiǎn shì dìsānzhě bǎoxiǎn háishì quánbǎo?** 你买的保险是第三者保险还是全保？
Could you sign here, please?	**Qǐng zài zhèlǐ qiān ge míng** 请在这里签个名

14.4 Theft

I've been robbed	**Wǒ bèi qiǎngjié le** 我被抢劫了
My...has been stolen	**Wǒde...bèi rén tōu le** 我的…被人偷了
My car's been broken into	**Wǒde qìchē bèi zéi qiàokāi le** 我的汽车被贼撬开了

14.5 Missing person

I've lost my child	**Wǒ de háizi diūshīle** 我的孩子丢失了
Could you help me find him/her?	**Nǐ néng bāng wǒ zhǎo tā ma?** 你能帮我找他／她吗？
Have you seen a lost child?	**Nǐ kànjiànguo yí ge mílù de xiǎohái ma?** 你看见过一个迷路的小孩吗？
He's/she's...years old	**Tā...suì** 他／她…岁
He/she's got...hair	**Tā de tóufa shì...sè de** 他／她的头发是…色的

short/long	**duǎn/cháng** 短 / 长
blond/red/brown/black/grey	**jīnsè/hóngsè/zōngsè/hēisè/huīsè** 金色 / 红色 / 棕色 / 黑色 / 灰色
curly/straight/frizzy	**juǎnfà/zhífà/xiǎojuǎnjié** 卷发 / 直发 / 小卷结
...in a ponytail	**shū mǎwěi de** 梳马尾的
...in braids	**shū biànzi de** 梳辫子的
...in a bun	**shū fàjì de** 梳发髻的
He's/she's got blue/brown/green eyes	**Tāde yǎnjing shì lánsè de/zōngsè de/lǜsè de** 他 / 她的眼睛是蓝色的 / 棕色的 / 绿色的
He/she's wearing...	**Tā chuānzhe** 他 / 她穿着…
swimming trunks/hiking boots	**yóuyǒng kùzi/lǚxíngxié** 游泳裤子 / 旅行鞋
with/without glasses	**dàizhe/méi dàizhe yǎnjìng** 戴着 / 没戴着眼镜
carrying/not carrying a bag	**shǒu názhe/méi názhe yí ge dàizi** 手拿着 / 没拿着一个袋子
He/She is tall/short	**Tā zhǎngdé gāo/ǎi** 他 / 她长得高 / 矮
This is a photo of him/her	**Zhè shì tāde zhàopiàn** 这是他 / 她的照片
He/she must be lost	**Tā yídìng shì mílù le** 他 / 她一定是迷路了

14.6 The police

An arrest

请给我你的驾驶证
Qǐng gěi wǒ nǐde jiàshǐzhèng

你超速了
Nǐ chāosùle

这里不能停放车辆
Zhèlǐ bùnéng tíngfàng chēliàng

你没有在计时器里投钱
Nǐ méiyǒu zài jìshíqì lǐ tóuqián

你的前灯／后灯不亮
Nǐ de qiándēng/hòudēng bú liàng

这驶…罚款
Zhè shǐ …fákuǎn

你想现在付款吗？
Nǐ xiǎng xiànzài fùkuǎn ma?

你得现在付款
Nǐ děi xiànzài fùkuǎn

Your (vehicle) documents, please

You were speeding

You're not allowed to park here

You haven't put money in the
  parking meter

Your front/rear lights aren't working

That's a ...fine

Do you want to pay now?

You'll have to pay now

I don't speak Chinese	**Wǒ búhuì shuō Hànyǔ/Zhōngwén** 我不会说汉语/中文
I didn't see the sign	**Wǒ méi kànjiàn biāozhì** 我没看见标志
I don't understand what it says	**Wǒ kànbudǒng shàngmiàn shuō shénme** 我看不懂上面说什么
I was only doing... kilometers an hour	**Wǒde sùdù měi xiǎoshí zhǐ shì…gōnglǐ** 我的速度每小时只是…公里
I'll have my car checked	**Wǒ mǎshàng qù xiūlǐ qìchē** 我马上去修理汽车
I was blinded by oncoming lights	**Kāiguòlái de chēdēng bǎ wǒde yǎnjīng nònghuāle** 开过来的车灯把我眼睛弄花了

At the police station

I want to report a collision/missing person/rape
Wǒ yào bào zhuàngchē/shīzōng/ qiángjiān de ànzi
我要报撞车／失踪／强奸的案子

Could you make a statement, please?
Nǐ néng zuò bǐgòng ma?
你能作笔供吗？

Could I have a copy for the insurance?
Wǒ néng yào yí fèn bǎoxiǎndān de fùběn ma?
我能要一份保险单的副本吗？

I've lost everything
Wǒ suǒyǒu de dōngxi dōu diūshī le
我所有的东西都丢失了

I've no money left, I'm desperate
Wǒde qián yě diū le, wǒ zǒu-tóu wú-lù le
我的钱也丢了，我走投无路了

Could you lend me a little money?
Nǐ néng jiè wǒ yìdiǎn qián ma?
你能借我一点钱吗？

I'd like an interpreter
Wǒ xūyào yí ge fānyì
我需要一个翻译

I'm innocent
Wǒ shì wúgū de
我是无辜的

I don't know anything about it
Zhè jiàn shì wǒ shénme dōu bù zhīdào
这件事我什么都不知道

I want to speak to someone from the American embassy
Wǒ yào gēn Měiguó Dàshǐguǎn de rén shuōhuà
我要跟美国大使馆的人说话

I want a lawyer who speaks...
Wǒ yào zhǎo yí ge huì shuō...de lǜshī
我要找一个会说…的律师

在哪里发生的？ **Zài nǎlǐ fāshēng de?**	Where did it happen?
什么时候发生的？ **Shénme shíhou fāshēng de?**	What time did it happen?
你丢失了什么？ **Nǐ diūshīle shénme?**	What's missing?
小偷拿了什么？ **Xiǎotōu nále shénme?**	What's been taken?

请给我看看你的身份证／护照
  **Qǐng gěi wǒ kànkan nǐde shēnfèn
  zhèng/hùzhào**
	Could I see your identity card/
	  passport?

有没有证人？ **Yǒu méiyǒu zhèngrén?**	Are there any witnesses?
请在这里签名 **Qǐng zài zhèlǐ qiānmíng**	Sign here, please
你需要翻译吗 **Nǐ xūyào fānyì ma?**	Do you want an interpreter?

15 English-Chinese Word List

English-Chinese Word List   176

15. English-Chinese Word List

The following word list is meant to supplement the chapters in this book. Some of the words not on this list can be found elsewhere in this book. Food items can be found in sections 4.7 and 4.8, and the parts of a car on pages 76-77 and the parts of a bicycle on pages 82-83.

A

abacus 算盘 **suànpán**

about (approximately) 大约 **dàyuē**

above 上面 **shàngmiàn**

abroad 国外 **guówài**

accident 事故 **shìgù**

acrobatics troupe 杂技团 **zájìtuán**

adapt (verb) 适应 **shìyìng**

adaptor 插座 **chāzuò**

address 地址 **dìzhǐ**

admission 入场 **rùchǎng**

admission price 入场费 / 门票费 **rùchǎngfèi/ménpiàofèi**

adult 成人 **chéngrén**

advice 建议 **jiànyì**

aerogram 航空邮件 **hángkōng yóujiàn**

after 在…以后 **zài...yǐhòu**

afternoon 下午 **xiàwǔ**

aftershave 须后水 **xūhòushuǐ**

again 再 **zài**

against 反对 **fǎnduì**

age 年龄 **niánlíng**

agree 同意 **tóngyì**

AIDS 艾滋病 **àizībìng**

air 空气 **kōngqì**

air conditioning 空调 **kōngtiáo**

air mattress 气垫 **qìdiàn**

air pollution 空气污染 **kōngqì wūrǎn**

airmail 航空邮件 **hángkōng yóujiàn**

airplane 飞机 **fēijī**

airport 飞机场 **fēijīchǎng**

alarm 警钟 **jǐngzhōng**

alarm clock 闹钟 **nàozhōng**

alcohol 酒 **jiǔ**

all day 全天 **quántiān**

all the time 总是 **zǒngshì**

allergy 过敏 **guòmǐn**

alone 单独 **dāndú**

also 也 **yě**

altogether 一共 **yígòng**

always 总是 **zǒngshì**

ambulance 救护车 **jiùhùchē**

America 美国 **Měiguó**

American (in general) 美国的 **Měiguó de**

American (people) 美国人 **Měiguórén**

amount 数量 **shùliàng**

amusement park 游乐场 **yóulèchǎng**

anaesthetic (general) 全身麻醉 **quánshēn mázuì**

anaesthetic (local) 局部麻醉 **júbù mázuì**

angry 生气 shēngqì

animal 动物 dòngwù

ankle 踝 huái

answer 回答 huídá

ant 蚂蚁 mǎyǐ

antibiotics 抗生素 kàngshēngsù

antique 古旧 gǔjiù

antiques 古玩 gǔwǎn

antiseptic 防腐剂 fángfùjì

anus 肛门 gāngmén

any 任何 rènhé

anyone 任何人 rènhé rén

apartment 公寓 gōngyù

apologies 道歉 dàoqiàn

apple 苹果 píngguǒ

apple juice 苹果汁 píngguǒzhī

appointment (meeting) 预约 yùyuē

April 四月 Sìyuè

architecture 建筑 jiànzhù

area 地区 dìqū

area code 区号 qūhào

argue 争吵 zhēngchǎo

arm 胳膊 gēbo

arrange 筹办 / 安排 chóubàn/ ānpái

arrive 到 dào

art 艺术 yìshù

artery 血管/动脉 xuèguǎn/ dòngmài

artificial respiration 人工呼吸 réngōng hūxī

arts and crafts 工艺美术 gōngyì měishù

ashtray 烟灰缸 yānhuīgāng

ask (verb) 问 wèn

ask for 要 yào

aspirin 阿司匹林 āsīpǐlín

asthma 哮喘 xiàochuǎn

at 在 zài

at home 在家 zài jiā

at night 晚上 wǎnshang

at the back 后面 hòumiàn

at the front 前面 qiánmiàn

at the latest 最迟 / 最晚 zuìchí/ zuìwǎn

August 八月 Bāyuè

Australia 澳大利亚 / 澳洲 Àodàlìyà/Àozhōu

Australian (in general) 澳大利亚的 / 澳洲的 Àodàlìyàde/ Àozhōude

Australian (people) 澳大利亚人/ 澳洲人 Àodàlìyàrén/Àozhōurén

automatic 自动的 zìdòngde

autumn 秋天 qiūtiān

avoid 避免 bìmiǎn

awake 醒 xǐng

B

baby 婴儿 yīng'ér

baby food 婴儿食品 yīng'ér shípǐn

babysitter 临时保姆 línshín bǎomǔ

back (part of body) 背 bèi

back (rear) 后面 hòumiàn

backpack 背包 bèibāo

backpacker 背包旅行者 bèibāo- lǚxíngzhě

bad (rotting) 臭 chòu

bad (terrible) 坏 / 糟 huài/zāo

bag 袋子 dàizi

baggage 行李 xíngli

ball 球 qiú

ballpoint pen 圆珠笔 yuán zhūbǐ

banana 香蕉 xiāngjiāo

Band Aid 创可贴 chuàngkětiē

bandage 绷带 bēngdài

bank (finance) 银行 yínháng

bank (river) 河岸 hé'àn

banquet 宴会 yànhuì
bar (cafè) 酒吧 jiǔbā
barbecue 烧烤 shāokǎo
barber 理发店 lǐ fàdiàn
bargain 讲价 jiǎngjià
baseball 棒球 bàngqiú
basketball 篮球 lánqiú
bath towel 浴巾 yùjīn
bathe 洗澡 xǐzǎo
bathmat 浴室防滑垫 yùshì
  fánghuádiàn
bathrobe 浴衣 yùyī
bathroom (bathing) 浴室 yùshì
bathroom (lavatory) 洗手间 /
  厕所 xǐshǒujiān/cèsuǒ
bathtub 浴缸 / 浴盆 yùgāng/
  yùpén
battery 电池 diànchí
beach 海滩 hǎitān
beancurd 豆腐 dòufu
beautiful 漂亮 / 美丽 piàoliang/
  měilì
beauty parlor 美容院
  měiróngyuàn
because 因为 yīnwèi
bed 床 chuáng
bedding 被褥 bèirù
bedroom 卧室 wòshì
beef 牛肉 niúròu
beer 啤酒 píjiǔ
before 以前 yǐqián
beggar 乞丐 qǐgài
begin 开始 kāishǐ
behind 在…后面 zài...hòumiàn
Beijing Opera 京剧 Jīngjù
below 在…下面 zài...xiàmiàn
belt 腰带 yāodài
berth 卧铺 wòpù
beside 在…旁边 zài...pángbiān
best 最好 zuì hǎo

better 比较好 bǐjiào hǎo
better (to get) 好转 hǎozhuǎn
between 在…之间 zài...zhījiān
bicycle 自行车 zìxíngchē
big 大 dà
bikini 三点式泳衣 / 比基尼
  sāndiǎnshì yǒngyī/bǐjīní
bill 帐单 zhàngdān
billiards 桌球 zhuōqiú
bird 鸟 niǎo
birthday 生日 shēngrì
biscuit 饼干 bǐnggān
bite 咬 yǎo
bitter 苦的 kǔde
black 黑色 hēisè
black and white 黑白 hēibái
black eye 青黑的眼睛 qīnghēi
  de yǎnjing
bland (taste) 单调 dāndiāo
blanket 毯子 tǎnzi
bleach (verb) 漂白 piàobái
bleed 流血 liúxuè
blind (can't see) 看不见
  kànbujiàn
blind (on window) 窗帘
  chuānglián
blister 水疱 shuǐpào
blog 博客 bókè
blond 金发 jīnfà
blood 血 xuè
blood pressure 血压 xuèyā
blood transfusion 输血 shūxuè
blouse 女衬衫 nǔ chènshān
blue 蓝色 lánsè
boarding gate 登机门 dēngjīmén
boat 船 chuán
body 身体 shēntǐ
boiled water 开水 kāishuǐ
bone 骨头 gǔtou
book 书 shū

booked, reserved 预订了 **yùdìngle**

booking office 订票处 **dìngpiàochù**

bookshop 书店 **shūdiàn**

border 边界 **biānjiè**

bored/boring 闷 / 无聊 **mèn/ wúliáo**

born 出生 **chūshēng**

borrow 借 **jiè**

botanic gardens 植物园 **zhíwùyuán**

both 两个 **liǎng ge**

bottle (baby's) 奶瓶 **nǎipíng**

bottle (wine) 瓶子 **píngzi**

bottle-warmer 暖瓶器 **nuǎnpíngqì**

bottle opener 开瓶器 **kāipíngqì**

bowl 碗 **wǎn**

box 盒子 **hézi**

box office 票房 **piàofáng**

boy 男孩儿 **nánháir**

boyfriend 男朋友 **nánpéngyou**

bra 乳罩 **rǔzhào**

bracelet 手镯 **shǒuzhuó**

braised 炒 **chǎo**

brake 刹车 **shāchē**

brake oil 刹车油 **shāchēyóu**

bread 面包 **miànbāo**

break (verb) 弄坏 **nònghuài**

breakfast 早饭 **zǎofàn**

breast 乳房 **rǔfáng**

breathe 呼吸 **hūxī**

bridge 桥 **qiáo**

bring 拿 **ná**

brochure 小册子 **xiǎocèzi**

broken 坏了 **huàile**

bronze 铜 / 青铜 **tóng/qīngtóng**

brothel 妓院 **jìyuàn**

brother 兄弟 **xiōngdì**

brown 褐色 / 棕色 **hèsè/zōngsè**

bruise 青肿 **qīngzhǒng**

brush 刷子 **shuāzi**

Buddhism 佛教 **Fójiào**

building 大楼 **dàlóu**

bulb 电灯泡 **diàndēngpào**

burglary 盗窃 **dàoqiè**

burn (injury) 烧伤 **shāoshāng**

burn (verb) 烧 **shāo**

bus 公共汽车 **gōnggòngqìchē**

bus stop 汽车站 **qìchēzhàn**

business 商业 **shāngyè**

business card 名片 **míngpiàn**

business class 头等舱 **tóuděngcāng**

business trip 出差 **chūchāi**

businessman 商人 **shāngrén**

busy (schedule) 忙 **máng**

busy (traffic) 拥挤 **yōngjǐ**

but 但是 **dànshì**

butter 黄油 **huángyóu**

button (for clothes) 扣子 **kòuzi**

button (to press) 按钮 **ànniǔ**

buy 买 **mǎi**

by airmail 航空 **hángkōng**

by phone 打电话 **dǎ diànhuà**

C

cabbage 卷心菜 **juǎnxīncài**

cabin 客舱 **kècāng**

cake 蛋糕 **dàn'gāo**

cake shop 糕点店 **gāodiǎndiàn**

call (name) 名叫 **míng jiào**

call (phone) 打电话 **dǎ diànhuà**

calligraphy 书法 **shūfǎ**

camera 照相机 **zhàoxiàngjī**

camping 野营 **yěyíng**

can (be able to) 能 / 可以 **néng/ kěyǐ**

can (tin of food) 罐头 **guàntóu**

can opener 罐头刀 **guàntóudāo**

cancel 取消 **qǔxiāo**

candle 蜡烛 **làzhú**

candy 糖果 **tángguǒ**

Cantonese 广州话 **Guǎngzhōuhuà**

car 汽车 **qìchē**

car seat (child's) 小孩座儿(汽车里的) **xiǎohái zuòr (qìchē lǐde)**

car trouble 汽车有毛病 **qìchē yǒu máobìng**

card 名片 **míngpiàn**

cardigan 毛衣 **máoyī**

care for 照顾 **zhàogu**

careful 小心 **xiǎoxīn**

carpet 地毯 **dìtǎn**

carriage 客车厢 **kèchēxiāng**

carrot 胡萝卜 **húluobo**

carry 提/带/载 **tí/dài/zài**

cash 现款 **xiànkuǎn**

cash a check 兑现 **duìxiàn**

cash machine 提款机 **tíkuǎnjī**

cashier 出纳员 **chū'nàyuán**

casino 赌场 **dǔchǎng**

cassette 盒式磁带 **héshì cídài**

cat 猫 **māo**

catalogue 目录 **mùlù**

cauliflower 花菜 **huācài**

cause 原因 **yuányīn**

cave 岩洞 **yándòng**

CD 光盘/光碟 **guāngpán/guāngdié**

CD-ROM 光盘阅读器 **guāngpán yuèdúqì**

celebrate 庆祝 **qìngzhù**

cemetery 墓地 **mùdì**

center (middle) 中间 **zhōngjiān**

center (of city) (市)中心 **(shì) zhōngxīn**

centigrade 摄氏 **shèshì**

centimeter 公分 **gōngfēn**

central heating 室内暖气 **shì'nèi nuǎnqì**

ceramics 陶器 **táoqì**

certificate 证书 **zhèngshū**

chair 椅子 **yǐzi**

champagne 香槟酒 **xiāngbīnjiǔ**

chance 机会 **jīhuì**

change (alter, vary) 改变 **gǎibiàn**

change (money) 零钱 **língqián**

change (swap) 交换 **jiāohuàn**

change (trains/buses) 转车 **zhuǎnchē**

change the baby's diaper 换尿布 **huàn niàobù**

charge (expense, cost) 费用 **fèiyòng**

charter flight 包租的班机 **bāozū de bānjī**

chat 聊天儿 **liáotiānr**

cheap 便宜 **piányi**

check (bill) 帐单 **zhàngdān**

check (money order) 支票 **zhīpiào**

check (verb) 检查 **jiǎnchá**

check in 登记 **dēngjí**

check out 退房 **tuìfáng**

checked luggage 检查行李 **jiǎnchá xíngli**

cheers! 干杯 **gānbēi**

cheese 乳酪/奶酪 **rǔlào/nǎilào**

chef 厨师 **chúshī**

chemist (pharmacy) 药店 **yàodiàn**

chess 国际象棋 **guójì xiàngqí**

chewing gum 香口糖 **xiāngkǒutáng**

chicken 鸡 **jī**

child 孩子 **háizi**

chilled 冰镇 **bīngzhèn**

chilli 辣椒 **làjiāo**

chin 下巴 **xiàbā**

China 中国 **Zhōngguó**

Chinese (in general) 中国的 **Zhōngguóde**

Chinese (language) 中文 / 汉语 **Zhōngwén/Hànyǔ**

Chinese (people) 中国人 **Zhōngguórén**

chocolate 巧克力 **qiǎokèlì**

choose 选择 **xuǎnzé**

chop (for name) 印章 **yìnzhāng**

chopsticks 筷子 **kuàzi**

church 教堂 **jiàotáng**

church service 礼拜 **lǐbài**

cigar 雪茄烟 **xuějiāyān**

cigarette 香烟 **xiāngyān**

circle (theater seats) 楼厅 **lóutīng**

circus 马戏 **mǎxì**

citizen 市民 / 公民 **shìmín/gōngmín**

city 城市 **chéngshì**

clean 干净 **gānjìng**

clean (verb) 弄干净 **nòng gānjìng**

clock 时钟 / 钟 **shízhōng/zhōng**

close 近 / 靠近 **jìn/kàojìn**

closed (shop, etc) 关门 **guānmén**

closed off (road) 封锁 **fēngsuǒ**

clothes, clothing 衣服 **yīfu**

clothes hanger 衣架 **yījià**

cloud 云 **yún**

coach (bus) 长途汽车 **chángtúqìchē**

coat (jacket) 外衣 **wàiyī**

coat (overcoat) 大衣 **dàyī**

cockroach 蟑螂 **zhānláng**

coffee 咖啡 **kāfēi**

cold (not hot) 冷 **lěng**

cold, flu 感冒 **gǎnmào**

collar 衣领 **yīlǐng**

colleague 同事 **tóngshì**

collision 撞车 **zhuàngchē**

cologne 男性香水 **nánxìng xiāngshuǐ**

color 颜色 **yánsè**

colored 带颜色的 **dài yánsè de**

comb 梳子 **shūzi**

come 来 **lái**

come back 回来 **huílai**

comedy 喜剧 **xǐjù**

comfortable 舒服 **shūfu**

company (business) 公司 **gōngsī**

compartment 分隔间（列车车厢的）**fēn'géjiān (lièchē chēxiāng de)**

complain 抱怨 **bàoyuàn**

complaint 投诉 **tóusù**

completely 全部 **quánbù**

complex 复杂 **fùzá**

computer 电脑 **diànnǎo**

comrade 同志 **tóngzhì**

concert 音乐会 **yīnyuèhuì**

concert hall 音乐厅 **yīnyuètīng**

condensed milk 炼奶 **liànnǎi**

condom 避孕套 **bìyùntào**

confectionery 糖果 **tángguǒ**

confirm 确认 **quèrèn**

congratulations! 祝贺你 **zhùhè nǐ**

connection (transport) 连接点 **liánjiēdiǎn**

constipation 便秘 **biànmì**

consulate 领事馆 **lǐngshìguǎn**

consultation (by doctor) 看病 / 就诊 **kànbìng/jiùzhěn**

contact lens 隐型眼镜 **yǐnxíng yǎnjìng**

contagious 传染的 **chuánrǎn de**

contraceptive 避孕 **bìyùn**

contraceptive pill 避孕药 **bìyùnyào**

contract 合同／契约 hétóng/qìyuē

convenient 方便 fāngbiàn

cook (person) 厨师 chúshī

cook (verb) 做菜 zuòcài

cookie 小甜饼 xiǎotiánbǐng

copper 铜／紫铜 tóng/zǐtóng

copy 副本 fùběn

copy (verb) 抄写／模仿 chāoxiě/mófǎng

corner 角落 jiǎoluò

correct 对／正确 duì/zhèngquè

correspond 通信 tōngxìn

corridor 走廊 zǒuláng

corrupt 腐败 fǔbài

cosmetics 化妆品 huàzhuāngpǐn

cost 成本 chéngběn

cost (price) 价格 jiàgé

costly 贵／昂贵 guì/ángguì

costume 民族服装／戏装 mínzú fúzhuāng/xìzhuāng

cot 婴儿床／童床 yīng'érchuáng/tóngchuáng

cotton 棉布 miánbù

cotton wool 棉花 miánhuā

cough 咳嗽声 késoushēng

cough (verb) 咳嗽 késou

cough lolly 咳嗽糖 késou táng

cough syrup 咳嗽药水 késou yàoshuǐ

count (verb) 数／算 shǔ/suàn

counter 柜台 guìtái

country (nation) 国家 guójiā

country (rural area) 乡下 xiāngxià

country code 国家区号 guójiā qūhào

course of treatment 疗程 liáochéng

cousin (children of father's brothers) 堂兄弟姐妹 tángxiōngdìjiěmèi

cousin (children of father's sisters and mother's siblings) 表兄弟姐妹 biǎoxiōngdìjiěmèi

cover (verb) 盖 gài

cow 母牛 mǔniú

crab 螃蟹 pángxiè

cramp (verb) 抽筋 chōujīn

crazy 疯狂的 fēngkuángde

credit card 信用卡 xìnyòngkǎ

crime 犯罪 fànzuì

cross (road, river) 越过 yuèguò

crossroads 十字路口 shízìlùkǒu

crutch 拐杖 guǎizhàng

cry 哭 kū

cubic meter 立方米 lìfāngmǐ

cucumber 黄瓜 huángguā

cuddly toy 引人搂抱的玩具 yǐnrén lǒubào de wánjù

cuff 袖口 xiùkǒu

cufflinks （衬衫袖口的）链扣 (chènshān xiùkǒu de) liànkòu

cup 杯子 bēizi

curly 卷曲的 juǎnqūde

current (electric) 电流 diànliú

curtains 窗帘 chuānglián

cushion 垫子 diànzi

custom 习俗 xísú

customer 顾客 gùkè

customs 海关 hǎiguān

cut (injury) 伤口 shāngkǒu

cut (verb) 切／割 qiē/gē

cutlery 刀叉餐具 dāochā cānjù

cycling 骑自行车 qí zìxíngchē

D

dad 爸爸 bàba

daily 日常的 rìchángde

dairy products 奶制品 nǎizhìpǐn

damage (verb) 损害 sǔnhài

dance (verb) 跳舞 tiàowǔ

dance 舞会 **wǔhuì**

dandruff 头皮 **tóupí**

danger 危险 **wēixiǎn**

dangerous 危险的 **wēixiǎn de**

dark 暗／黑暗 **àn/hēi'àn**

date 日期 **rìqī**

date of birth 出生日期
chūshēng rìqī

daughter 女儿 **nǚ'ér**

day 天 **tiān**

day after tomorrow 后天 **hòutiān**

day before yesterday 前天
qiántiān

dead 死了 **sǐ le**

deaf 聋的 **lóngde**

decaffeinated 无咖啡因的
wúkāfēiyīn de

deceive 欺骗 **qīpiàn**

December 十二月 **Shí'èryuè**

decide 决定 **juédìng**

declare (customs) 报关 **bàoguān**

deep 深 **shēn**

deep freeze 急冻 **jídòng**

degrees 度 **dù**

delay 耽搁 **dān'ge**

delicious 好吃 **hǎochī**

deliver 运送 **yùnsòng**

democracy 民主 **mínzhǔ**

dentist 牙医 **yáyī**

dentures 假牙 **jiǎyá**

deny 否认 **fǒurèn**

deodorant 除体臭液
chútǐchòuyè

department store 百货商店
bǎihuòshāngdiàn

departure 出发 **chūfā**

departure time 起程时间
qǐchéng shíjiān

deposit (for safekeeping) 押金
yājīn

deposit (in bank) 存款 **cúnkuǎn**

desert 沙漠 **shāmò**

dessert 甜食 **tiánshí**

destination 目的地 **mùdìdì**

destroy 破坏 **pòhuài**

detergent 去垢剂 **qùgòujì**

develop (photo) 冲洗 **chōngxǐ**

diabetic 糖尿病 **tángniàobìng**

dial (phone) 拨（电话） **bō**
(diànhuà)

diamond 钻石 **zuànshí**

diaper 纸尿布 **zhǐniàobù**

diarrhea 泻肚子 **xiè dùzi**

dictionary 词典 **cídiǎn**

diesel oil 柴油 **cháiyóu**

diet 饮食 **yǐnshí**

different 不同 **bùtóng**

difficulty 困难 **kùnnan**

dim sum 港式点心 **gǎngshì**
diǎnxīn

dining car 餐车 **cānchē**

dining room 餐厅 **cāntīng**

dinner 晚饭 **wǎnfàn**

direct flight 直航 **zhíháng**

direction 方向 **fāngxiàng**

directly 直接 **zhíjiē**

dirty 脏 **zāng**

disabled 残疾人 **cánjirén**

disappointment 失望 **shīwàng**

disco 迪斯科 **dísīkē**

discount 优惠 **yōuhuì**

dish 盘子 **pánzi**

dish of the day 今天推荐的菜
jīntiān tuījiàn de cài

disinfectant 消毒剂 **xiāodújì**

dislocate 脱臼 **tuōjiù**

dissatisfied 不满意 **bù mǎnyì**

distance 距离 **jùlí**

distilled water 蒸馏水
zhēngliúshuǐ

disturb 打扰 **dǎrǎo**

disturbance 骚乱 **sāoluàn**

divorced 离婚 **líhūn**

dizzy 头晕 **tóuyūn**

do 做 **zuò**

do not disturb 请勿打扰 **qǐng wù dǎrǎo**

doctor 医生 / 大夫 **yīshēng/dàifu**

dog 狗 **gǒu**

doll 娃娃 **wáwa**

domestic 国内 **guónèi**

door 门 **mén**

double 双倍 **shuāngbèi**

double bed 双人床 **shuāngrénchuáng**

down 下 **xià**

downstairs 楼下 **lóuxià**

draught 穿堂风 **chuāntángfēng**

dream 梦 **mèng**

dream (verb) 做梦 **zuòmèng**

dress (verb) 穿 **chuān**

dress 连衣裙 **liányīqún**

dress up 穿扮 **chuānbàn**

dressing gown 晨衣 **chényī**

dressing table 梳妆台 **shūzhuāngtái**

drink (alcoholic) 带酒精的饮料 **dài jiǔjīng de yǐnliào**

drink (refreshment) 饮料 **yǐnliào**

drink (verb) 喝 **hē**

drinking water 饮用水 **yǐnyòngshuǐ**

drive (verb) 开车 **kāichē**

driver 司机 **sījī**

driver's license 驾驶证 **jiàshǐzhèng**

drug (medicine) 药 **yào**

drug (recreational) 毒品 **dúpǐn**

drugstore 药店 **yàodiàn**

drunk 喝醉 **hēzuì**

dry 干 **gān**

dry (verb) 弄干 **nònggān**

dry-clean 干洗 **gānxǐ**

drycleaners 干洗店 **gānxǐdiàn**

duck 鸭子 **yāzi**

dumpling 饺子 **jiǎozi**

during 在···期间 **zài...qījiān**

during the day 白天 **báitiān**

dust 灰尘 **huīchén**

duty (tax) 关税 **guānshuì**

duty-free goods 免税品 **miǎnshuìpǐn**

duty-free shop 免税店 **miǎnshuìdiàn**

DVD 数据录像机 **shùjù lùxiàngjī**

dynasty 朝代 **cháodài**

E

each 每 **měi**

each other 互相 **hùxiāng**

ear 耳朵 **ěrduo**

ear drops 耳药水 **ěryàoshuǐ**

earache 耳朵疼 **ěrduo téng**

early 早 **zǎo**

earn 赚 **zhuàn**

earrings 耳环 **ěrhuán**

earthquake 地震 **dìzhèn**

east 东边 **dōngbiān**

easy 容易 **róngyì**

eat 吃 **chī**

economy 经济 **jīngjì**

economy class 经济舱 **jīngjìcāng**

egg 鸡蛋 **jīdàn**

eggplant 茄子 **qiézi**

eight 八 **bā**

eighteen 十八 **shíbā**

eighty 八十 **bāshí**

electric fan 电风扇 **diànfēngshàn**

electricity 电 **diàn**

electronic 电子 **diànzi**

elephant 大象 dàxiàng

elevator 电梯 diàntī

eleven 十一 shíyī

email 电子邮件 / 依妹儿 diànzi yóujiàn/yīmèir

embarrassed 难为情 nánwéiqíng

embassy 大使馆 dàshǐguǎn

embroidery 刺绣 cìxiù

emergency 急诊 jízhěn

emergency brake 紧急刹车 jǐnjí shāchē

emergency exit 紧急出口 jǐnjí chūkǒu

emperor 皇帝 huāngdì

empress 皇后 huānghòu

empty 空的 kōngde

end 完 wán

England 英国 Yīngguó

English (in general) 英国的 Yīngguóde

English (language) 英文 / 英语 Yīngwén/Yīngyǔ

English (person) 英国人 Yīngguórén

enjoy 享受 xiǎngshòu

enough 足够 zúgòu

enquire 问 wèn

enter 进入 jìnrù

entire 全部 quánbù

entrance 入口 rùkǒu

envelope 信封 xìnfēng

equality 平等 píngděng

escalator 电动楼梯 diàndòng lóutī

especially 特别 tèbié

essential 重要 zhòngyào

evening 晚上 wǎnshang

evening wear 晚装 wǎnzhuāng

every 每 měi

everybody 每个人 měi ge rén

everything 一切 yíqiè

everywhere 到处 dàochù

examine 检查 jiǎnchá

example 例子 lìzi

excellent 优秀的 yōuxiù de

exchange (money) 兑换 duìhuàn

exchange rate 兑换率 duìhuànlǜ

excursion 短途旅行 duǎntú lǚxíng

excuse me 请问 qǐngwèn

exhausted 累坏了 lèihuàile

exhibition 展览 zhǎnlǎn

exit 出口 chūkǒu

expenses 费用 fèiyòng

expensive 贵 guì

explain 解释 jiěshì

export 出口 chūkǒu

express (letter) 快递 kuàidì

express (train) 特快 tèkuài

external use 外用的 wàiyòng de

extension cord 接长电线 jiēcháng diànxiàn

eye 眼睛 yǎnjing

eye drops 眼药水 yǎnyàoshuǐ

eye specialist 眼科医生 yǎnkē yīshēng

F

fabric 布料 bùliào

face 脸 liǎn

factory 工厂 gōngchǎng

Fahrenheit 华氏 Huáshì

faint 昏厥 hūnjué

fall (season) 秋天 qiūtiān

fall (verb) 倒下来 dǎoxiàlái

false 假的 jiǎde

family 家庭 jiātíng

famous 有名 yǒumíng

fan 扇子 shànzi

far away 很远 hěn yuǎn

fare 票价 piào jià

farm 农场 **nóngcǎng**

farmer 农夫 **nóngfū**

fashion show 时装表演
shízhuāng biǎoyǎn

fast 快 **kuài**

fat 胖 **pàng**

father 父亲 / 爸爸 **fùqin/bàba**

father-in-law 岳父 **yuèfù**

fault 过错 **guòcuò**

fax 传真 **chuánzhēn**

February 二月 **Èryuè**

feel 觉得 **juéde**

feel like 想要 **xiǎng yào**

fence 篱笆 **líbā**

ferry 渡船 **dùchuán**

festival 节日 **jiérì**

fever 发烧 **fāshāo**

few 极少 / 几个 **jíshǎo/jǐge**

few (number) 几个 **jǐ ge**

fiancè 未婚夫 **wèihūnfū**

fiancèe 未婚妻 **wèihūnqī**

fifteen 十五 **shíwǔ**

fifty 五十 **wǔshí**

fill (verb) 装满 **zhuāngmǎn**

fill out (form) 填表 **tiánbiǎo**

filling (dental) 填充物
tiánchōngwù

film (cinema) 电影 **diànyǐng**

film (photo) 胶卷 **jiāojuǎn**

filter (lens) 滤光气 **lǜguāngqì**

filter cigarette 香烟过滤嘴
xiāngyān guòlǜzuǐ

find 找 **zhǎo**

fine (money) 罚款 **fákuǎn**

fine food 美餐 **měicān**

finger 手指 **shǒuzhǐ**

finish 完成 **wánchéng**

fire 失火 **shīhuǒ**

fire alarm 火警 **huǒjǐng**

fire department 消防局
xiāofángjú

fire escape 安全梯 **ānquántī**

fire extinguisher 灭火器
mièhuǒqì

first 第一 **dìyī**

first aid 急救 **jíjiù**

first class 头等 **tóuděng**

fish 鱼 **yú**

fish (verb) 钓鱼 **diàoyú**

fishing rod 鱼竿 **yúgān**

fitness club 健身俱乐部
jiànshēn jùlèbù

fitness training 健身锻炼
jiànshēn duànliàn

fitting room 试衣室 **shìyīshì**

five 五 **wǔ**

fix 修理 **xiūlǐ**

flag 旗 **qí**

flash (camera) 闪光灯
shǎnguāngdēng

flashlight 手电筒 **shǒudiàntǒng**

flavor 味道 **wèidào**

flight 班机 **bānjī**

flight number 班机号 **bānjīhào**

flood 洪水 **hóngshuǐ**

floor 楼 / 层 **lóu/céng**

flour 面粉 **miànfěn**

flu 感冒 **gǎnmào**

flush 冲洗 **chōngxǐ**

fly (insect) 苍蝇 **cāngyíng**

fly (verb) 飞 **fēi**

fog 雾 **wù**

foggy 下雾 **xiàwù**

folklore 民俗 **mínsú**

follow 跟随 **gēnsuí**

food (groceries) 食物 **shíwù**

food (meal) 饭菜 **fàncài**

food poisoning 进食中毒 **jìnshí
zhòngdú**

foot (anatomy) 脚 **jiǎo**

football (soccer) 足球 **zúqiú**

forbidden 禁止 **jìnzhǐ**

foreign 外国的 **wàiguó de**

foreign exchange 外汇 **wàihuì**

forget 忘记 **wàngjì**

fork 叉子 **chāzi**

form 表格 **biǎogé**

formal dress 夜礼服 **yèlǐfú**

forty 四十 **sìshí**

forward 向前 **xiàng qián**

four 四 **sì**

France 法国 **Fǎguó**

free (no charge) 免费 **miǎnfèi**

free (unoccupied) 有空儿 **yǒu kòngr**

free time 空儿 **kòngr**

freedom 自由 **zìyóu**

freeze 结冰 **jiébīng**

French (in general) 法国的 **Fǎguóde**

French (language) 法语／法文 **Fǎyǔ/Fǎwén**

French (people) 法国人 **Fǎguórén**

french fries 炸薯条 **zháshǔtiáo**

fresh 新鲜 **xīnxiān**

Friday 星期五 **Xīngqīwǔ**

fried 油炸 **yóuzhá**

friend 朋友 **péngyou**

friendly 友好 **yǒuhǎo**

frightened 被吓着 **bèixiàzhe**

fringe (hair) 前刘海儿 **qián liúhǎir**

from 从 **cóng**

front 前面 **qiánmiàn**

frozen 冰冻 **bīngdòng**

fruit 水果 **shuǐguǒ**

fruit juice 果汁 **guǒzhī**

frying pan 煎锅 **jiān'guō**

full 满 **mǎn**

fun 好玩儿 **hǎowánr**

funeral 葬礼 **zànglǐ**

funny 好笑 **hǎoxiào**

G

game 游戏 **yóuxì**

garage (car repair) 修车行 **xiūchēxíng**

garbage 垃圾 **lājī**

garden 花园 **huāyuán**

garlic 大蒜 **dàsuàn**

garment 衣服 **yīfu**

gas station 加油站 **jiāyóuzhàn**

gasoline 汽油 **qìyóu**

gate 大门 **dàmén**

gem 宝石 **bǎoshí**

gender 性别 **xìngbié**

genuine 真的 **zhēnde**

German (language) 德语／德文 **Déyǔ/Déwén**

German (in general) 德国的 **Déguó de**

German (people) 德国人 **Déguórén**

Germany 德国 **Déguó**

get off (boat) 下船 **xiàchuán**

get off (bus, train) 下车 **xiàchē**

get on (boat) 上船 **shàngchuán**

get on (bus, train) 上车 **shàngchē**

gift 礼物 **lǐwù**

ginger 姜 **jiāng**

girl 女孩儿／姑娘 **nǚháir/gūniang**

girlfriend 女朋友 **nǚpéngyou**

give 给 **gěi**

given name 名字 **míngzi**

glass (for drinking) 杯子 **bēizi**

glass (material) 玻璃 **bōlí**

glasses 眼镜 **yǎnjìng**

glossy (photo) 光面的 **guāngmiàn de**

gloves 手套 shǒutào

glue 胶水 jiāoshuǐ

go 去 qù

go back 回去 huíqù

go out 出去 chūqù

gold 金 jīn

golf 高尔夫球 gāo'ěrfūqiú

golf course 高尔夫球场 gāo'ěrfū qiúchǎng

good afternoon 你好 nǐ hǎo

good evening 晚上好 wǎnshàng hǎo

good morning 早上好 zǎoshang hǎo

good night 晚安 wǎn'ān

goodbye 再见 zàijiàn

gram 克 kè

grandchild 孙子 sūnzǐ

granddaughter 孙女 sūnnǚ

grandfather (maternal) 外祖父／姥爷 wàizǔfù/lǎoye

grandfather (paternal) 祖父／爷爷 zǔfù/yéye

grandmother (maternal) 外祖母／姥姥 wàizǔmǔ/lǎolao

grandmother (paternal) 祖母／奶奶 zǔmǔ/nǎinai

grandparent (maternal) 外祖父母 wàizǔfùmǔ

grandparent (paternal) 祖父母 zǔfùmǔ

grandson 孙儿 sūn'ér

grapes 葡萄 pútao

grave 坟墓 fénmù

gray 灰色 huīsè

gray-haired 灰白 huībái

graze (injury) 擦破处 cāpòchù

greasy (food) 油腻 yóunì

Great Wall 长城 Chángchéng

green 绿色 lǜsè

green tea 绿茶 lǜchá

greengrocer 蔬菜水果店 shūcài-shuǐguǒdiàn

greeting 打招呼 dǎ zhāohu

grilled 烧烤 shāokǎo

groceries 杂货 záhuò

grocery 杂货店 záhuòdiàn

group 团体 tuántǐ

guide (book) 旅游指南 lǚyóu zhǐnán

guide (person) 导游 dǎoyóu

guided tour 解说的参观 jiěshuō de cānguān

guilty 有罪 yǒuzuì

gym 健身房 jiànshēnfáng

gynecologist 妇科医生 fùkē yīshēng

H

hair 头发 tóufa

hairbrush 梳子 shūzi

haircut 理发 lǐfà

hairdresser 理发师 lǐfàshī

hairdryer 吹风机 chuīfēngjī

hairspray 定型胶 dìngxíngjiāo

hairstyle 发型 fàxíng

half 一半 yíbàn

half full 半满 bànmǎn

ham 火腿 huǒtuǐ

hand 手 shǒu

hand brake 手闸 shǒuzhá

hand luggage 手提行李 shǒutí xíngli

hand towel 手巾 shǒujīn

handbag 手提包 shǒutíbāo

handkerchief 手绢儿 shǒujuànr

handmade 手工制的 shǒugōngzhì de

handsome 英俊 yīngjùn

hanger 衣架 yījià

happy 开心, 高兴 kāixīn, gāoxìng

harbor 港口 **gǎngkǒu**

hard (difficult) 难 **nán**

hard (firm) 硬 **yìng**

hard seat (train) 硬座 **yìngzuò**

hard sleeper (train) 硬卧 **yìngwò**

hat 帽子 **màozi**

have 有 **yǒu**

have to 必需 **bìxū**

hay fever 花粉热 **huāfěnrè**

he 他 **tā**

head 头 **tóu**

headache 头疼 **tóuténg**

headlights 前灯 **qiándēng**

healthy 健康 **jiànkāng**

hear 听见 **tīngjiàn**

hearing aid 助听器 **zhùtīngqì**

heart 心脏 **xīnzàng**

heart attack 心脏病 **xīnzàngbìng**

heat 暖气 **nuǎnqì**

heater 暖炉 **nuǎnlú**

heavy 重 **zhòng**

heel (of foot) 脚后跟 **jiǎohòugēn**

heel (of shoe) 后跟 **hòugēn**

height 高度 **gāodù**

height (body) 身高 **shēn'gāo**

hello 你好 **Nǐ hǎo**

help (assist) 帮助 / 帮忙 **bāngzhù/bāngmáng**

Help! (for emergency) 救命阿！ **jiùmìng ā!**

helping (of food) （食物的）一份 **(shíwù de) yífèn**

here 这里 / 这儿 **zhèlǐ/zhèr**

high 高 **gāo**

high chair 高椅 **gāoyǐ**

high tide 高潮 **gāocháo**

highway 公路 **gōnglù**

hiking 徒步旅行 **túbù lǚxíng**

hire 租 **zū**

history 历史 **lìshǐ**

hitchhike 搭车 **dāchē**

hobby 爱好 **àihào**

holiday (festival) 节日 **jiérì**

holiday (public) 假日 **jiàrì**

holiday (vacation) 度假 **dùjià**

homesick 想家 **xiǎngjiā**

homosexual 同性恋 **tóngxìngliàn**

honest 诚实的 **chéngshí de**

honey 蜂蜜 **fēngmì**

hope 希望 **xīwàng**

horrible 可怕的 **kěpà de**

hors d'oeuvres 开胃菜 **kāiwèicài**

horse 马 **mǎ**

hospital 医院 **yīyuàn**

hospitality 好客 **hàokè**

hot (spicy) 辣 **là**

hot (warm) 热 **rè**

hot spring 温泉 **wēnquán**

hot water 热水 **rèshuǐ**

hot-water bottle 暖水袋 **nuǎnshuǐdài**

hotel 旅馆 / 宾馆 **lǚguǎn/ bīn'guǎn**

hour 小时 / 钟头 **xiǎoshí/ zhōngtóu**

house 房子 **fángzi**

how? 怎么 **zěnme**

how far? 多远？ **Duō yuǎn?**

how long? 多长？ **Duō cháng?**

how many? 多少 / 几个？ **Duōshao/jǐ ge?**

how much? 多少钱 **Duōshao qián?**

humid 潮湿 **cháoshī**

hundred 百 **bǎi**

hungry 饿 **è**

hurry (pressed) 急 **jí**

hurry (quickly) 赶快 **gǎnkuài**

husband 丈夫 **zhàngfū**

I

I 我 **wǒ**

ice 冰 **bīng**

ice cream 冰激凌 / 冰淇淋
bīngjīlíng/bīngqílín

ice-skating 滑冰 **huábīng**

idea 主意 **zhǔyì**

identification (card) 身份证
shēnfènzhèng

identify 身份 **shēnfèn**

idiot 白痴 **báichī**

if 如果 / 要是 **rúguǒ/yàoshi**

ill 有病的 **yǒubìng de**

illegal 非法 **fēifǎ**

illness 病 **bìng**

imagine 想象 **xiǎngxiàng**

immediately 立刻 / 马上 **lìkè/
mǎshàng**

immigration/arrival 入境 **rùjìng**

important 重要 **zhòngyào**

impossible 不可能 **bù kěnéng**

improve 改进 **gǎijìn**

in 在…里 **zài…lǐ**

in the evening （在）晚上 **(zài)
wǎnshang**

in the morning （在）早上 **(zài)
zǎoshàng**

increase 增加 **zēngjiā**

included 包括在内 **bāokuò zài
nèi**

including 包括 **bāokuò**

income 收入 **shōurù**

indicate 指示 **zhǐshì**

indicator (car) 指示器 **zhǐshìqì**

indigestion 消化不良 **xiāohuà
bù liáng**

inexpensive 便宜 **piányi**

infected 感染 **gǎnrǎn**

infectious 传染 **chuánrǎn**

inflammation 发炎 **fāyán**

inflation 通货膨胀 **tōnghuò
péngzhàng**

information 信息 **xìnxī**

information desk 询问处 **xún-
wèn chù**

injection 打针 **dǎzhēn**

injured 受伤 **shòushāng**

innocent 无辜 **wúgū**

insect 虫子 **chóngzǐ**

insect bite 虫咬 **chóng yǎo**

insect repellent 驱虫剂
qūchóngjì

inside 在…里 **zài …lǐ**

instead of 代替 **dàitì**

instructions 说明 **shuōmíng**

insurance 保险 **bǎoxiǎn**

intelligent 聪明 **cōngmíng**

interested 感兴趣 **gǎn xìngqù**

interesting 有趣 **yǒuqù**

internal use (medicine) 内服
nèifú

international 国际 **guójì**

Internet 互联网 / 网络
Hùliánwǎng/wǎngluò

Internet cafe, cybercafe 网吧
Wǎngbā

interpreter 翻译 / 口译员 **fānyì/
kǒuyìyuán**

intersection 十字路口 **shízìlùkǒu**

introduce 介绍 **jièshào**

introduce oneself 自我介绍
zìwǒ jièshào

invite 邀请 **yāoqǐng**

invoice 发票 **fāpiào**

Ireland 爱尔兰 **Ài'ěrlán**

iron (for clothes) 熨斗 **yùndǒu**

iron (metal) 铁 **tiě**

iron (verb) 熨 **yùn**

island 岛 **dǎo**

Italian (in general) 意大利的
Yìdàlìde

Italian (language) 意大利语 Yìdàlìyǔ

Italian (people) 意大利人 Yìdàlìrén

Italy 意大利 Yìdàlì

itchy 痒 yǎng

itinerary 日程表 rìchéngbiǎo

J

jack (for car) 千斤顶 qiānjīndǐng

jack (verb) 顶起 dǐngqǐ

jacket 外套 wàitào

jade 玉 yù

jam 果酱 guǒjiàng

January 一月 Yīyuè

Japan 日本 Rìběn

Japanese (in general) 日本的 Rìběnde

Japanese (language) 日文／日语 Rìwén/Rìyǔ

Japanese (people) 日本人 Rìběnrén

jasmine tea 茉莉花茶 mòlì huāchá

jazz 爵士音乐 juéshì yīnyuè

jeans 牛仔裤 niúzǎikù

jellyfish 水母 shuǐmǔ

jewelry 珠宝／首饰 zhūbǎo/shǒushì

jewelry shop 珠宝店 zhūbǎodiàn

job 工作 gōngzuò

jog 跑步 pǎobù

joke 笑话 xiàohuà

journalist 记者 jìzhě

journey 路途 lùtú

juice 果汁 guǒzhī

July 七月 Qīyuè

jumper 毛衣 máoyī

June 六月 Liùyuè

just (only) 只 zhǐ

just (very recently) 刚才 gāngcái

K

keep 留 liú

kerosene 煤油 méiyóu

key 钥匙 yàoshi

kilogram 公斤 gōngjīn

kilometer 公里 gōnglǐ

king 国王 guówáng

kitchen 厨房 chúfáng

knee 膝盖 xīgài

knife 刀子 dāozi

knit 打毛衣 dǎ máoyī

know (facts) 知道 zhīdào

know (people) 认识 rènshi

L

laces (for shoes) 鞋带 xiédài

lake 湖 hú

lamb (mutton) 羊肉 yángròu

lamp 灯 dēng

land (ground) 地 dì

land (verb) 着陆 zhuólù

landscape 风景 fēngjǐng

lane (of traffic) 路线 lùxiàn

language 语言 yǔyán

large 大 dà

last (endure) 持续 chíxù

last (final) 最后 zuìhòu

last night 昨晚 zuówǎn

late 晚 wǎn

late in arriving 迟到 chídào

later 过一会儿 guò yìhuǐr

laugh 笑 xiào

launderette 洗衣店 xǐyīdiàn

laundry soap 洗衣粉 xǐyīfěn

law 法律 fǎlǜ

lawyer 律师 lǜshī

laxative 轻泻剂 qīngxièjì

lazy 懒惰 lǎnduò

leaded petrol 含铅汽油 hánqiān qìyóu

leak 漏水 lòushuǐ
learn 学 xué
leather 皮革 pígé
leave 离开 líkāi
leave (train/bus) 开车 kāichē
least 最少 zuìshǎo
least (at least) 至少/起码 zhìshǎo/qǐmǎ
left (direction) 左边 zuǒbiān
left behind 留下 liúxià
leg 腿 tuǐ
legal 合法 héfǎ
leisure 空闲 kōngxián
lemon 柠檬 níngméng
lend 借 jiè
lens (camera) 镜头 jìngtóu
less 少一点儿 shǎo yìdiǎnr
letter 信 xìn
letter-writing paper 信纸 xìnzhǐ
lettuce 莴苣 wōjù
library 图书馆 túshūguǎn
license 执照 zhízhào
lie (be lying) 说谎 shuōhuǎng
lie (falsehood) 谎话 huǎnghuà
lie down 躺下 tǎngxià
lift (elevator) 电梯 diàntī
light (lamp) 灯 dēng
light (not dark) 亮 liàng
light (not heavy) 轻 qīng
light bulb 灯泡 dēngpào
lighter 打火机 dǎhuǒjī
lightning 闪电 shǎndiàn
like (verb) 喜欢 xǐhuan
linen 床单 chuángdān
lip 嘴唇 zuǐchún
lipstick 口红 kǒuhóng
listen 听 tīng
liter 升 shēng
little (amount) 一点儿 yìdiǎnr

little (small) 小 xiǎo
live (alive) 活着 huózhe
live (verb) 生活 shēnghuó
liver 肝 gān
lobster 龙虾 lóngxiā
local 本地 běndì
lock 锁 suǒ
long 长 cháng
long-distance call 长途电话 chángtú diànhuà
look at 看 kàn
look for 找 zhǎo
look up 查 chá
lose (not win) 输 shū
loss 损失 sǔnshī
lost (can't find way) 迷路 mílù
lost (missing) 丢了 diūle
lost and found office 失物招领处 shīwù zhāolǐngchù
loud 大声 dàshēng
love 爱情 àiqíng
love (verb) 爱 ài
low 低 dī
low tide 低潮 dīcháo
LPG 煤气／石油气 méiqì/shíyóuqì
luck 运气 yùnqì
luggage 行李 xínglǐ
luggage locker 行李存柜 xínglǐ cúnguì
lunch 午饭 wǔfàn
lungs 肺 fèi
lychees 荔枝 lìzhī

M
magazine 杂志 zázhì
mail (letters) 信 xìn
mail (verb) 寄 jì
mailbox 邮筒 yóutǒng
main 主要 zhǔyào

main road 主干路 zhǔgànlù

make, create 做／制造 zuò/zhìzào

make an appointment 预约 yùyuē

make love 做爱 zuò'ài

makeshift 临时凑合 línshí còuhé

makeup 化妆品 huàzhuāngpǐn

man 男人 nánrén

manager 经理 jīnglǐ

Mandarin (language) 普通话／国语 Pǔtōnghuà/Guóyǔ

manicure 修甲 xiūjiǎ

many 很多 hěnduō

map 地图 dìtú

March 三月 Sānyuè

marital status 婚姻状态 hūnyīn zhuàngtài

market 市场 shìchǎng

married 已婚 yǐhūn

massage 按摩 ànmó

match 比赛 bǐsài

matches 火柴 huǒchái

matte (photo) 绸面的 chóu-miànde

mattress 床垫 chuángdiàn

May 五月 Wǔyuè

maybe 也许 yěxǔ

meal 餐 cān

meaning 意思 yìsi

measure (verb) 量 liáng

meat 肉 ròu

medicine 药 yào

meet 见面 jiànmiàn

meeting 会议 huìyì

mend 修补 xiūbǔ

menu 菜单 càidān

merchant 商人 shāngrén

message 留言／便条 liúyán/biàntiáo

metal 金属 jīnshǔ

metal detector 金属探测门 jīnshǔ tàncè mén

meter (in taxi) 计程器 jìchéngqì

meter (measure) （一）米／公尺 (yī) mǐ/gōngchǐ

method 方法 fāngfǎ

midday 中午 zhōngwǔ

middle 中间 zhōngjiān

midnight 午夜 wǔyè

migraine 偏头痛 piāntóutòng

mild (climate) 温暖的 wēnnuǎn de

milk 牛奶 niúnǎi

millimeter 毫米 háomǐ

million 百万 bǎiwàn

mine 我的 wǒde

mineral water 矿泉水 kuàngquánshuǐ

minute 分(钟) fēn (zhōng)

mirror 镜子 jìngzi

miss (flight, train) 没赶上 méi gǎnshàng

Miss (term of address) 小姐 xiǎojie

miss (think of) 想念 xiǎngniàn

missing 失踪了 shīzōngle

missing person 失踪者 shīzōngzhě

mist 薄雾 bówù

misty 有薄雾 yǒu bówù

mistake 错误 cuòwù

mistaken 弄错 nòngcuò

misunderstanding 误会 wùhuì

modern 现代的 xiàndàide

Monday 星期一 Xīngqīyī

money 钱 qián

monkey 猴子 hóuzi

month 月 yuè

moon 月亮 yuèliang

moped 机动自行车 jīdòng zìxíngchē

morning 早上 zǎoshang

more 多一点儿 duō yìdiǎnr

mosquito 蚊子 wénzi

mosquito net 蚊帐 wénzhàng

mother 妈妈／母亲 māma/mǔqīn

mother-in-law 岳母 yuèmǔ

motorbike 摩托车 mótuōchē

mountain 山 shān

mouse 小老鼠 xiǎolǎoshǔ

mouth 嘴 zuǐ

move (heavy object) 搬 bān

movie 电影 diànyǐng

Mr (term of address) 先生 xiānsheng

Mrs (term of address) 太太 tàitai

MSG 味精 wèijīng

much 许多 xǔduō

mud 泥 ní

muscle 肌肉 jīròu

museum 博物馆 bówùguǎn

mushrooms 蘑菇 mógu

music 音乐 yīnyuè

musical instrument 乐器 yuèqì

Muslim 清真／穆斯林／回教 Qīngzhēn/Mùsīlín/Huíjiào

must 必须 bìxū

mutton 羊肉 yángròu

my 我的 wǒde

N

nail (finger) 指甲 zhǐjiǎ

nail (metal) 钉子 dīngzi

nail clippers 指甲钳 zhǐjiǎqián

nail file 指甲锉 zhǐjiǎcuò

nail scissors 指甲剪 zhǐjiǎjiǎn

napkin 餐巾 cānjīn

napkin, sanitary 月经带 yuèjīngdài

nappy, diaper 尿布 niàobù

nationality 国籍 guójí

natural 自然的 zìránde

nature 自然界 zìránjiè

nauseous 作呕 zuò'ǒu

near 离…近 lí…jìn

nearby 附近 fùjìn

necessary 必需 bìxū

neck 脖子 bózi

necklace 项链 xiàngliàn

necktie 领带 lǐngdài

needle 针 zhēn

neighbor 邻居 línjū

nephew (son of father's brothers) 侄子／侄儿 zhízi/zhí'ér

nephew (son of father's sisters) 外甥 wàishēng

nephew (son of wife's siblings) 外甥 wàishēng

never 从来没有 cónglái méiyǒu

new 新 xīn

news 新闻 xīnwén

news stand 报亭 bàotíng

newspaper 报 bào

next 下一个 xià yí ge

next to 旁边 pángbiān

nice 好 hǎo

niece (daughter of father's brothers) 侄女 zhínǚ

niece (daughter of father's sisters) 外甥女 wàishēngnǚ

niece (daughter of wife's siblings) 外甥女 wàishēngnǚ

night 夜里 yèlǐ

night view 夜景 yèjǐng

nightclub 夜总会 yèzǒnghuì

nine 九 jiǔ

nineteen 十九 shíjiǔ

ninety 九十 jiǔshí

nipple (bottle) 象皮奶头 xiàngpí nǎitóu

no 不是 **búshì**

no entry 不准驶入 **bùzhǔn shǐrù**

no one 没有人 **méiyǒu rén**

no thank you 谢谢, 我不要 **xièxie, wǒ búyào**

noise 嘈杂声／噪音 **cáozáshēng/zàoyīn**

noisy 嘈杂的 **cáozáde**

non-stop (flight) 直航 **zhíháng**

noodles 面条 **miàntiáo**

noon 中午 **zhōngwǔ**

normal 正常的 **zhèngchángde**

north 北边 **běibiān**

nose 鼻子 **bízi**

nose drops 鼻药水 **bíyàoshuǐ**

nosebleed 鼻出血 **bí chūxiě**

notebook 笔记本 **bǐjìběn**

notepad 信纸 **xìnzhǐ**

nothing 没有东西 **méiyǒu dōngxi**

novel 小说 **xiǎoshuō**

November 十一月 **Shíyīyuè**

now 现在 **xiànzài**

number 号码 **hàomǎ**

number plate 车牌号码 **chēpái hàomǎ**

nurse 护士 **hùshì**

O

obvious 明显 **míngxiǎn**

occupation 职业 **zhíyè**

October 十月 **Shíyuè**

of course 当然 **dāngrán**

off (gone bad) 坏了 **huàile**

off (turned off) 关上 **guānshàng**

office 办公室 **bàn'gōngshì**

oil 油 **yóu**

ointment 药膏 **yàogāo**

okay 行 **xíng**

old (used for people) 老 **lǎo**

old (used for things) 旧 **jiù**

Olympics 奥林匹克运动会／奥运会 **Àolínpǐkè Yùndònghuì/Àoyùnhuì**

on, at 在…上 **zài...shàng**

on (turned on) 开 **kāi**

on the left 在…左边 **zài...zuǒbiān**

on the right 在…右边 **zài...yòubiān**

on the way 快到了 **kuài dào le**

once 一次 **yí cì**

one 一 **yī**

one-way ticket 单程票 **dānchéngpiào**

one-way traffic 单程路 **dānchénglù**

onion 洋葱 **yángcōng**

online chat 在线上聊天 **zài xiàn shàng liáotiān**

only 只有 **zhǐyǒu**

open 开门 **kāimén**

open (verb) 打开 **dǎkāi**

opera 歌剧 **gējù**

operate (surgeon) 做手术 **zuò shǒushù**

operator (telephone) 总机 **zǒngjī**

opportunity 机会 **jīhuì**

opposite 对面 **duìmiàn**

optician 眼镜商 **yǎnjìngshāng**

orange (color) 橙色 **chéngsè**

orange (fruit) 桔子 **júzi**

order (meal) 点菜 **diǎncài**

ordinary 普通的 **pǔtōng de**

other 别的／其他的 **biéde/qítāde**

other (alternative) 另外 **lìngwài**

our 我们的 **wǒmende**

outside 外面 **wàimiàn**

over there 那边 **nàbiān**

overseas 国外 **guówài**

overtake (vehicle) 超车 **chāochē**

owe 欠 **qiàn**

P

packed lunch 饭盒 **fànhé**

packet 包 **bāo**

page 页 **yè**

pagoda 宝塔 **bǎotǎ**

pain 痛 **tòng**

painkiller 止痛药 **zhǐtòngyào**

painting 画儿／绘画 **huàr/ huìhuà**

pair 一双 **yì shuāng**

pajamas 睡衣 **shuìyī**

palace 宫殿 **gōngdiàn**

pan 锅 **guō**

panties 紧身短衬裤 **jǐnshēn duǎnchènkù**

pants 裤子 **kùzi**

pantyhose 袜裤 **wàkù**

paper 纸 **zhǐ**

parcel 包裹 **bāoguǒ**

parents 父母 **fùmǔ**

park, gardens 公园 **gōngyuán**

parking space 停车位子 **tíngchē wèizi**

partner 伴侣／伙伴 **bànlǚ/ huǒbàn**

party (event) 聚会 **jùhuì**

passenger 乘客 **chéngkè**

passport 护照 **hùzhào**

passport number 护照号码 **hùzhào hàomǎ**

pay (verb) 付钱 **fùqián**

pay the bill 付账／买单 **fùzhàng/mǎidān**

peach 桃子 **táozi**

peanut 花生米 **huāshēng mǐ**

pear 梨 **lí**

pearl 珍珠 **zhēnzhū**

peas 豌豆 **wāndòu**

pedestrian crossing 人行横道 **rénxíng héngdào**

pen 钢笔 **gāngbǐ**

pencil 铅笔 **qiānbǐ**

penis 阴茎 **yīnjīng**

penknife 小刀 **xiǎodāo**

people 人 **rén**

pepper (black) 胡椒 **hújiāo**

pepper (chilli) 辣椒 **làjiāo**

performance 演出 **yǎnchū**

perfume 香水 **xiāngshuǐ**

perhaps 也许 **yěxǔ**

period (menstrual) 月经期 **yuèjīng qī**

permit 许可证 **xǔkě zhèng**

permit (verb) 许／准许 **xǔ/ zhǔnxǔ**

person 人 **rén**

personal 私人的 **sīrénde**

perspire 出汗 **chūhàn**

petrol 汽油 **qìyóu**

petrol station 加油店 **jiāyóudiàn**

pharmacy 药店 **yàodiàn**

phone 电话 **diànhuà**

phone (verb) 打电话 **dǎ diànhuà**

phone booth 公用电话亭 **gōngyòng diànhuàtíng**

phone card 电话磁卡 **diànhuà cíkǎ**

phone directory 电话本 **diànhuàběn**

phone number 电话号码 **diànhuà hàomǎ**

photo 照片 **zhàopiàn**

photocopier 复印机 **fùyìnjī**

photocopy (verb) 复印 **fùyìn**

phrasebook 短语集 **duǎnyǔjí**

pick up (someone) 接 **jiē**

picnic 野餐 **yěcān**

pill (contraceptive) 避孕药 **bìyùnyào**

pillow 枕头 **zhěntou**

pillowcase 枕套 **zhěntào**

pills, tablets 药丸／药片 **yàowán/yàopiàn**

pin 大头针 **dàtóuzhēn**

pineapple 波萝 **bōluó**

pink 粉红色 **fěnhóngsè**

pity 可惜 **kěxī**

place 地方 **dìfang**

place of interest 名胜 **míngshèng**

plain (simple) 朴素 **pǔsù**

plan (intention) 打算 **dǎsuàn**

plan (map) 略图 **lüètú**

plane 飞机 **fēijī**

plant 植物 **zhíwù**

plastic 塑料 **sùliào**

plastic bag 塑料袋 **sùliàodài**

plate 盘子 **pánzi**

platform 月台／站台 **yuètái/ zhàntái**

play (drama) 话剧 **huàjù**

play (verb) 玩儿 **wánr**

play golf 打高尔夫球 **dǎ gāo'ěrfūqiú**

play tennis 打网球 **dǎ wǎngqiú**

playground 运动场 **yùndòngchǎng**

playing cards 朴克牌 **pùkèpái**

please 请 **qǐng**

plug (electric) 插头 **chātóu**

plum 李子 **lǐzi**

pocket 口袋 **kǒudài**

pocketknife 小折刀 **xiǎozhédāo**

point out 指出 **zhǐchū**

poisonous 有毒的 **yǒudúde**

police 警察 **jǐngchá**

police station 公安局／警察局 **gōng'ān jú/jǐngchájú**

pond 池塘 **chítáng**

pool 游泳池 **yóuyǒngchí**

poor (not rich) 穷 **qióng**

poor (pitiful) 可怜 **kělián**

population 人口 **rénkǒu**

porcelain 瓷器 **cíqì**

pork 猪肉 **zhūròu**

porter (for bags) 服务员 **fúwùyuán**

possible 可能 **kěnéng**

post (verb) 寄 **jì**

post office 邮局 **yóujú**

postage 邮费 **yóufèi**

postbox 邮筒 **yóutǒng**

postcard 明信片 **míngxìnpiàn**

postcode 邮政编码 **yóuzhèng biānmǎ**

postpone 延期 **yánqī**

potato 土豆 **tǔdòu**

potato chips 炸薯条 **zháshǔtiáo**

poultry 家禽 **jiāqín**

powdered milk 奶粉 **nǎifěn**

practice 练习 **liànxí**

prawn 虾 **xiā**

precious stone 宝石 **bǎoshí**

prefer 更喜欢 **gèng xǐhuan**

preference 喜爱 **xǐ'ài**

pregnant 怀孕 **huáiyùn**

prepare 准备 **zhǔnbèi**

prescription 药方 **yàofāng**

present (gift) 礼物 **lǐwù**

present (here) 现在 **xiànzài**

pressure 压力 **yālì**

pretty 漂亮 **piàoliang**

price 价钱 **jiàqián**

price list 价格表 **jiàgébiǎo**

print (picture) 照片 **zhàopiàn**

print (from computer) 打印 **dǎyìn**

print (develop photo) （晒）印 **(shài) yìn**

private 私人的 **sīrénde**

probably 大概 **dàgài**

problem 问题 **wèntí**

product 产品 **chǎnpǐn**

profession 职业 zhíyè
profit 利润 lìrùn
program 节目 jiémù
promise 答应 dāyìng
pronounce 发音 fāyīn
prostitute 妓女 jìnǚ
protect 保护 bǎohù
province 省 shěng
public 公共 gōnggòng
pull 拉 lā
pull a muscle 扯伤肌肉
  chěshāng jīròu
purchase 买 mǎi
pure 纯的 chúnde
purple 紫色 zǐsè
purse (for money) 钱包 qiánbāo
purse (handbag) 手袋 shǒudài
push 推 tuī
put 放 fàng
pyjamas 睡衣 shuìyī

Q

quality 质量 zhìliàng
quantity 数量 shùliàng
quarrel 吵架 chǎojià
quarter 四分之一 sìfēnzhīyī
quarter of an hour 一刻钟
  yíkèzhōng
queen 王后 wánghòu
question 问题 wèntí
queue 排队 páiduì
quick 快 kuài
quiet 安静 ānjìng
quilt 被子 bèizi

R

rabbit 兔子 tùzi
radio 收音机 shōuyīnjī
railway 铁路 tiělù

railway station 火车站
  huǒchēzhàn
rain 雨 yǔ
rain (verb) 下雨 xiàyǔ
raincoat 雨衣 yùyī
rape 强奸 qiángjiān
rapids 急流 jíliú
rare 难得 nándé
rash 疹子 zhěnzi
rat 耗子／老鼠 hàozi/lǎoshǔ
raw 生的 shēngde
razor blade 剃刀片 tìdāopiàn
read 看书 kànshū
ready 准备好了 zhǔnbèihǎole
really 实际 shíjì
reason 原因 yuányīn
receipt 收据 shōujù
receive 收到 shōudào
reception desk 服务台 fúwùtái
recommend 推荐 tuījiàn
rectangle 长方形 chángfāngxíng
red 红色 hóngsè
red wine 红葡萄酒／红酒 hóng
  pútaojiǔ/hóngjiǔ
reduction 降价 jiàngjià
refrigerator 冰箱 bīngxiāng
refund 退款 tuìkuǎn
refuse 拒绝 jùjué
regards 问候 wènhòu
region 地区 dìqū
registered 挂号 guàhào
registered mail 挂号邮件
  guàhào yóujiàn
regret 遗憾 yíhàn
relatives 亲戚 qīnqi
reliable 可靠 kěkào
religion 宗教 zōngjiào
remember 记得 jìde
rent/hire 租 zū
repair 修 xiū

repeat 重复 **chóngfù**

report (police) 报警 **bàojǐng**

represent 代表 **dàibiǎo**

reserve 保留 **bǎoliú**

responsible 负责 **fùzé**

rest 休息 **xiūxi**

restaurant 饭馆 **fànguǎn**

restroom 洗手间 **xǐshǒujiān**

result 结果 **jiéguǒ**

retired 退休 **tuìxiū**

return (come back) 回来 **huílái**

return (give back) 还 **huán**

return (go back) 回去 **huíqù**

return ticket 来回票 **láihuípiào**

reverse charges 对方付费
　duìfāng fùfèi

rheumatism 风湿病 **fēngshībìng**

ribbon 丝带 **sīdài**

rice (cooked) 米饭 **mǐfàn**

rice (grain) 大米 **dàmǐ**

ridiculous 可笑的 **kěxiàode**

riding (horseback) 骑马 **qímǎ**

right (correct) 正确 **zhèngquè**

right (side) 右边 **yòubiān**

right of way 优先 **yōuxiān**

ring 戒指 **jièzhǐ**

rinse 冲洗 **chōngxǐ**

ripe 熟的 **shúde**

risk 冒险 **màoxiǎn**

river 河 **hé**

road 路 **lù**

roadway 车行道 **chēxíngdào**

roasted 烘烤 **hōngkǎo**

rock (stone) 石头 **shítou**

roof 屋顶 **wūdǐng**

room 房间 **fángjiān**

room number 房间号码
　fángjiān hàomǎ

room service 房间服务 **fángjiān
　fúwù**

rope 绳子 **shéngzi**

round 圆形的 **yuánxíngde**

route 路线 **lùxiàn**

rowing boat 划艇 **huátǐng**

rubber (eraser) 橡皮擦 **xiàngpícā**

rubber (material) 橡胶 **xiàngjiāo**

rude 无礼的 **wúlǐde**

ruins 遗迹 **yíjī**

run (verb) 跑 **pǎo**

running shoes 赛跑鞋 **sàipǎoxié**

S

sad 难过 **nánguò**

safe 安全 **ānquán**

safe (for cash) 保险箱
　bǎoxiǎnxiāng

safety pin 别针 **biézhēn**

salad 沙拉 **shālā**

sale 出售 **chūshòu**

sales clerk 售货员 **shòuhuòyuán**

salt 盐 **yán**

same 一样 **yíyàng**

sandals 凉鞋 **liángxié**

sandy beach 沙滩 **shātān**

sanitary towel 月经带 **yuèjīngdài**

satisfied 满意 **mǎnyì**

Saturday 星期六 **xīngqīliù**

sauce 调味汁 **tiáowèizhī**

saucepan 平底锅 **píngdǐguō**

sauna 桑那浴 **sāngnàyù**

say 说 **shuō**

scald (injury) 烫伤 **tàngshāng**

scales 秤／天平 **chèng/tiānpíng**

scarf 围巾 **wéijīn**

scarf (headscarf) 头巾 **tóujīn**

scenery 自然风景 **zìrán
　fēngjǐng**

schedule 时刻表／日程表
　shíkèbiǎo/rìchéngbiǎo

school 学校 **xuéxiào**

scissors 剪刀 **jiǎndāo**

screwdriver 起子／螺丝刀 **qǐzi/ luósīdāo**

sculpture 雕塑 **diāosù**

sea 海 **hǎi**

seafood 海鲜 **hǎixiān**

season 季节 **jìjié**

seat 座位 **zuòwèi**

second (in line) 第二个 **dì'èr ge**

second (instant) 秒 **miǎo**

sedative 镇静剂 **zhènjìngjì**

see 看见 **kànjiàn**

seem 似乎 **sìhū**

send (fax) 发 **fā**

send (post) 寄 **jì**

sentence 句子 **jùzi**

separate 分开 **fēnkāi**

September 九月 **Jiǔyuè**

serious 严肃 **yánsù**

serious (injury) 严重 **yánzhòng**

service 服务 **fúwù**

seven 七 **qī**

seventeen 十七 **shíqī**

seventy 七十 **qīshí**

sew 缝 **fèng**

shade 阴凉处 **yīnliángchù**

shallow 浅 **qiǎn**

shampoo 洗发剂 **xǐfàjì**

shark 鲨鱼 **shāyú**

shave (verb) 刮胡子 **guā húzǐ**

shaver 电动剃刀 **diàndòng tìdāo**

shaving cream 修面霜 **xiūmiànshuāng**

she, her 她 **tā**

sheet 被单 **bèidān**

shirt 衬衫／衬衣 **chènshān/ chènyī**

shoe 鞋 **xié**

shoe polish 鞋油 **xiéyóu**

shop, store 商店 **shāngdiàn**

shop (verb) 购物 **gòuwù**

shop assistant 营业员 **yíngyèyuán**

shop window 橱柜 **chúguì**

shopping center 购物中心 **gòuwù zhōngxīn**

short (height) 矮 **ǎi**

short (length) 短 **duǎn**

shorts (short trousers) 短裤 **duǎnkù**

shoulder 肩膀 **jiānbǎng**

show to 给…看 **gěi...kàn**

shower (for washing) 淋浴 **línyù**

shower (rain) 阵雨 **zhènyǔ**

shrimp 小虾 **xiǎoxiā**

shuttle bus 接驳车 **jiēbóchē**

shy 害羞 **hàixiū**

sightseeing 观光 **guān'guāng**

sign (road) 路标 **lùbiāo**

sign (verb) 签名 **qiānmíng**

signature 签名 **qiānmíng**

silk 丝绸 **sīchóu**

silver 银 **yín**

simple 简单 **jiǎndān**

since (until now) 自从 **zìcóng**

sing 唱歌 **chànggē**

single (only one) 单一 **dānyī**

single (unmarried) 单身 **dānshēn**

single ticket 单程票 **dānchéngpiào**

sir 先生 **xiānsheng**

sister (older) 姐姐 **jiějie**

sister (younger) 妹妹 **mèimei**

sit 坐 **zuò**

six 六 **liù**

sixteen 十六 **shíliù**

sixty 六十 **liùshí**

size 大小 **dàxiǎo**

size (clothes) 尺寸 **chǐcùn**

skiing 滑雪 **huáxuě**

skin 皮肤 pífū

skirt 裙子 qúnzi

sky 天空 tiānkōng

sleep 睡觉 shuìjiào

sleeping car 卧铺 wòpù

sleeping pills 安眠药 ānmiányào

sleepy 困 kùn

sleeve 袖子 xiùzi

slippers 拖鞋 tuōxié

slow 慢 màn

small 小 xiǎo

small change 零钱 língqián

smelly 臭味 chòuwèi

smile 笑 xiào

smoke (verb) 抽烟 chōuyān

smoke detector 烟火指示器 yānhuǒ zhǐshìqì

snack 小吃 xiǎochī

snake 蛇 shé

snow 雪 xuě

snow (verb) 下雪 xiàxuě

soap 肥皂 féizào

soap powder 皂粉 zàofěn

soccer 足球 zúqiú

soccer match 足球赛 zúqiúsài

socialism 社会主义 shèhuìzhǔyì

socket (electric) 插座 chāzuò

socks 袜子 wàzi

soft 软 ruǎn

soft drink 汽水 qìshuǐ

soft seat 软座 ruǎnzuò

soft sleeper 软卧 ruǎnwò

software 软件 ruǎnjiàn

soil 泥土 nítǔ

sole (of shoe) 鞋底 xiédǐ

some 一些 yìxiē

someone 有人 yǒurén

something 什么 shénme

sometimes 有时 yǒushí

somewhere 某处 mǒuchù

son 儿子 érzi

song 歌 gē

soon 不久 bùjiǔ

sore (painful) 痛／酸痛 tòng/suāntòng

sore (ulcer) 伤口 shāngkǒu

sore throat 喉咙疼 hóulóngténg

sorry 对不起, 抱歉 duìbuqǐ, bàoqiàn

soup 汤 tāng

sour 酸 suān

south 南边 nánbian

souvenir 纪念品 jìniànpǐn

soy sauce (salty) 咸酱油 xián jiàngyóu

soy sauce (sweet) 甜酱油 tián jiàngyóu

space 空间／地方 kōngjiān/dìfang

speak 讲／说 jiǎng/shuō

special 特别 tèbié

specialist (doctor) 专科医生 zhuānkē yīshēng

specialty (cooking) 好菜 hǎocài

speed limit 限定的速度 xiàndìngde sùdù

spell 用字母拼 yòng zìmǔ pīn

spend money 花钱 huāqián

spices 香料 xiāngliào

spicy 加香料的／辛辣的 jiā xiāngliào de/xīnlà de

spider 蜘蛛 zhīzhū

spoon 汤匙／汤勺 tāngchí/tāng sháo

sport 体育运动 tǐyù yùndòng

sports center 体育中心 tǐyù zhōngxīn

spouse 配偶 pèiǒu

sprain 扭伤 niǔshāng

spring (season) 春天 chūntiān

square (plaza) 广场 **guǎngchǎng**

square (shape) 正方形 **zhèngfāngxíng**

square meter 平方米 **píngfāngmǐ**

stadium 体育场 **tǐyùchǎng**

stain 污点 **wūdiǎn**

stain remover 去污剂 **qùwūjì**

stairs 楼梯 **lóutī**

stale 不新鲜 **bù xīnxiān**

stamp 邮票 **yóupiào**

stand up 站起来 **zhànqǐlái**

star 星星 **xīngxīng**

start 开始 **kāishǐ**

station 站 **zhàn**

statue 雕像 **diāoxiàng**

stay overnight 留宿／过夜 **liúsù/guòyè**

steal 偷 **tōu**

steamed 蒸的 **zhēngde**

stepfather 继父 **jìfù**

stepmother 继母 **jìmǔ**

steps 台阶 **táijiē**

sterilize 消毒 **xiāodú**

sticky tape 胶带 **jiāodài**

stockings 长筒袜子 **cháng tǒng wàzi**

stomach (abdomen) 肚子 **dùzi**

stomach (organ) 胃 **wèi**

stomach ache 肚子痛 **dùzi tòng**

stools 凳子 **dèngzi**

stop (bus) 站 **zhàn**

stop (cease) 停 **tíng**

stop (halt) 站住 **zhànzhù**

stopover 中途停留 **zhōngtú tíngliú**

store, shop 商店 **shāngdiàn**

storm 风暴 **fēngbào**

story (building) 层／楼 **céng/lóu**

straight 直的 **zhíde**

straight ahead 一直走 **yìzhí zǒu**

strange 奇怪 **qíguài**

straw (drinking) 吸管 **xīguǎn**

street 街 **jiē**

street vendor 小贩 **xiǎofàn**

strike (work stoppage) 罢工 **bàgōng**

string 绳子 **shéngzi**

strong 强壮 **qiángzhuàng**

study (room) 书房 **shūfáng**

study (verb) 学／学习 **xué/xuéxí**

stupid 笨／蠢 **bèn/chǔn**

sturdy 结实 **jiēshi**

subtitles 字幕 **zìmù**

suburb 郊区 **jiāoqū**

subway 地铁 **dìtiě**

succeed 成功 **chénggōng**

sugar 糖 **táng**

suit 一套西服 **yí tào xīfú**

suitcase 箱子 **xiāngzi**

suite 套房 **tàofáng**

summer 夏天 **xiàtiān**

sun 太阳 **tàiyáng**

Sunday 星期天／星期日 **Xīngqītiān/Xīngqīrì**

sunglasses 墨镜 **mòjìng**

sunrise 日出 **rìchū**

sunscreen 防晒油 **fángshàiyóu**

sunset 日落 **rìluò**

sunshade 阳伞 **yángsǎn**

supermarket 超级市场 **chāojí shìchǎng**

sure 一定 **yídìng**

surface mail 海／陆邮寄 **hǎi/lù yóujì**

surname 姓 **xìng**

surprise 惊奇 **jīngqí**

swallow (verb) 吞 **tūn**

swamp 沼泽地 **zhǎozédì**

sweat (verb) 出汗 **chūhàn**

sweater 毛衣 **máoyī**

sweet 甜 **tián**

swim (verb) 游泳 **yóuyǒng**

swimming costume 游泳衣
yóuyǒngyī

swimming pool 游泳池
yóuyǒngchí

switch (light) 电灯开关
diàndēng kāiguān

swollen 肿了 **zhǒngle**

syrup 糖浆 **tángjiāng**

T

table 桌子 **zhuōzi**

table tennis 乒乓球
pīngpāngqiú

tablecloth 桌布 **zhuōbù**

tablemat 垫子 **diànzi**

tablespoon 大汤匙 **dà tāngchí**

tablets 药片 **yàopiàn**

tableware 餐具 **cānjù**

tailor's 裁缝店 **cáiféng diàn**

take (medicine) 吃药 **chīyào**

take (photograph) 照相 **zhào-
xiàng**

take (time) 需要时间 **xūyào
shíjiān**

takeaway 带走 **dàizǒu**

talk 谈话 **tánhuà**

tall 高 **gāo**

tampon 卫生棉条
wèishēngmiántiáo

Taoism 道教 **Dàojiào**

tap 水龙头 **shuǐlóngtóu**

tap water 非饮用水 **fēi
yǐnyòngshuǐ**

tape measure 软尺 **ruǎnchǐ**

tape recorder 录音机 **lùyīnjī**

taste (flavor) 味道 **wèidào**

taste (style) 趣味 **qùwèi**

taste (verb) 尝 **cháng**

tasty 好吃 **hǎochī**

tax 税 **shuì**

tax-free shop 免税店 **miǎnshuì
diàn**

taxi 出租汽车 **chūzūqìchē**

taxi stand 出租汽车站
chūzūqìchēzhàn

tea (black) 不加奶的茶 **bù jiā
nǎi de chá**

tea (green) 绿茶 **lǜchá**

tea house 茶楼 **chálóu**

teacup 茶杯 **chábēi**

teapot 茶壶 **cháhú**

teaspoon 茶勺 **chásháo**

teat (bottle) 象皮奶头 **xiàngpí
nǎitóu**

telephoto lens 望远镜头
wàngyuǎn jìngtóu

television 电视 **diànshì**

tell 告诉 **gàosu**

temperature (body) 体温 **tǐwēn**

temperature (heat) 温度 **wēndù**

temple 寺院 **sìyuàn**

temporary 暂时 **zànshí**

tender, sore 脆弱的 **cuìruòde**

tennis 网球 **wǎngqiú**

tennis court 网球场
wǎngqiúchǎng

ten 十 **shí**

ten thousand 万 **wàn**

tent 帐篷 **zhàngpeng**

terminal 航站 **hángzhàn**

terminus 终点站 **zhōngdiǎnzhàn**

thank 感谢 **gǎnxiè**

thank you, thanks 谢谢 **xièxie**

that 那(个) **nà (ge)**

thaw (verb) 解冻 **jiědòng**

theater 剧院 **jùyuàn**

theft 偷盗 **tōudào**

their 他们的 **tāmende**

there 那边 **nàbiān**

there is (are) 有 **yǒu**

thermometer (body) 体温计 **tǐwēnjì**

thermometer (weather) 温度计 **wēndùjì**

they 他们 **tāmen**

thick 厚 **hòu**

thief 贼 **zéi**

thigh 大腿 **dàtuǐ**

thin (not fat) 瘦 **shòu**

thin (not thick) 薄 **bó**

thing 东西 **dōngxi**

think (believe) 相信 **xiāngxìn**

think (ponder) 想 / 考虑 **xiǎng/ kǎolǜ**

third (in a series) 第三 **dìsān**

third (1/3) 三分之一 **sānfēnzhīyī**

thirsty 渴 **kě**

this 这(个) **zhè (ge)**

this afternoon 今天下午 **jīntiān xiàwǔ**

this evening 今天晚上 **jīntiān wǎnshàng**

this morning 今天早上 **jīntiān zǎoshang**

thousand 千 **qiān**

thread 线 **xiàn**

three 三 **sān**

throat 喉咙 **hóulóng**

throat lozenges 润喉糖 **rùnhóutáng**

through (passage) 经过 **jīngguò**

thunder (verb) 打雷 **dǎléi**

thunderstorm 雷暴雨 **léibàoyǔ**

Thursday 星期四 **Xīngqīsì**

ticket (admission) 入场券 **rùchǎngquàn**

ticket (travel) 票 **piào**

ticket office 售票处 **shòupiàochù**

tide 潮水 **cháoshuǐ**

tidy 整齐 **zhěngqí**

tie (necktie) 领带 **lǐngdài**

tie (verb) 系 **jì**

tights (pantyhose) 袜裤 **wàkù**

tights (thick) 紧身衣裤 **jǐnshēn yīkù**

time 时间 **shíjiān**

time (occasion) 次 **cì**

times (multiplying) 乘 **chéng**

timetable 时刻表 **shíkèbiǎo**

tin (can) 罐头 **guàntou**

tin opener 罐头刀 **guàntoudāo**

tip (gratuity) 小费 **xiǎofèi**

tire 轮胎 **lúntāi**

tired 累 **lèi**

tissues (facial) 纸巾 **zhǐjīn**

toast (bread) 烤面包 **kǎo miànbāo**

toast (with drinks) 干杯 **gānbēi**

tobacco 烟草 **yāncǎo**

today 今天 **jīntiān**

toddler 学走的小孩 **xué zǒu de xiǎohái**

toe 脚趾 **jiǎozhǐ**

together 一起 **yìqǐ**

toilet 厕所 / 洗手间 **cèsuǒ/ xǐshǒujiān**

toilet (seated) 坐厕 **zuòcè**

toilet (squat) 蹲厕 **dūncè**

toilet bowl 抽水马桶 **chōushuǐ mǎtǒng**

toilet paper 卫生纸 **wèishēngzhǐ**

toilet seat 马桶座圈 **mǎtǒng zuòquān**

toiletries 梳妆用品 **shūzhuāng yòngpǐn**

tomato 西红柿 **xīhóngshì**

tomb 陵墓 **língmù**

tomorrow 明天 **míngtiān**

tongue 舌头 **shétou**

tonight 今晚 jīnwǎn

too 太 tài

tool 工具 gōngjù

tooth 牙 yá

toothache 牙疼 yáténg

toothbrush 牙刷 yáshuā

toothpaste 牙膏 yágāo

toothpick 牙签 yáqiān

top 顶 dǐng

top up 加满 jiāmǎn

torch, flashlight 手电筒 shǒudiàntǒng

total 一共 yígòng

touch 摸 mō

tour 参观 cānguān

tour group 旅行团 lǚxíngtuán

tour guide 导游 dǎoyóu

tourist class 经济舱 jīngjìcāng

toward 向 xiàng

towel 毛巾 máojīn

tower 塔 tǎ

town 市镇 shìzhèn

toy 玩具 wánjù

trade 贸易 màoyì

traffic 交通 jiāotōng

traffic light 红绿灯 hónglǜdēng

train 火车 huǒchē

train station 火车站 huǒchēzhàn

train ticket 火车票 huǒchēpiào

train timetable 火车时刻表 huǒchē shíkèbiǎo

transfer (bank) 过户 guòhù

translate (verb) 翻译/笔译 fānyì/bǐyì

translator 翻译者 fānyìzhě

travel 旅行 lǚxíng

travel agent 旅行社 lǚxíngshè

traveler 旅游者／旅客 lǚyóuzhě/lǚkè

traveler's check 旅行支票 lǚxíng zhīpiào

traveling bag 旅行包 lǚxíngbāo

treatment 治疗 zhìliáo

tree 树 shù

triangle 三角形 sānjiǎoxíng

trim (haircut) 修剪 xiūjiǎn

trip 旅行／旅程 lǚxíng/lǚchéng

trouble 麻烦 máfan

trousers 裤子 kùzi

truck 卡车 kǎchē

true 真的 zhēnde

trustworthy 可信的 kěxìnde

try 试 shì

try on 试穿 shìchuān

Tuesday 星期二 Xīngqī'èr

tunnel 隧道 suìdào

turn (change direction) 转 zhuǎn

turn off 关上 guānshang

turn on 开 kāi

TV 电视 diànshì

TV guide 电视指南 diànshì zhǐnán

tweezers 镊子 nièzi

twelve 十二 shí'èr

twice 两次 liǎng cì

Twitter 推特 tuītè

two (measure) 两 liǎng

two (numeral) 二 èr

typhoon 台风 táifēng

U

ugly 难看／丑 nánkàn/chǒu

ulcer 溃疡 kuìyáng

umbrella 伞 sǎn

under 在…底下 zài...dǐxia

underground (subway) 地铁 dìtiě

underpants 内裤 nèikù

15

understand 懂 **dǒng**
underwear 内衣 **nèiyī**
undress 脱衣服 **tuō yīfú**
unemployed 失业 **shīyè**
uneven 不平坦 **bù píngtǎn**
university 大学 **dàxué**
unleaded petrol 无铅汽油 **wúqiān qìyóu**
until 直到 **zhídào**
up 上 **shàng**
upset (unhappy) 烦闷 **fánmèn**
upset stomach 胃不舒服 **wèi bù shūfú**
upstairs 楼上 **lóushàng**
urgent 紧急 **jǐnjí**
urine 尿 **niào**
urinate (verb) 小便 **xiǎobiàn**
us 我们 **wǒmen**
use 用 **yòng**
used up 用完了 **yòngwánle**
useful 有用的 **yǒuyòngde**
useless 无用的 **wúyòngde**
usually 通常 **tōngcháng**

V

vacancy 空房 **kōngfáng**
vacant 空的 **kōngde**
vacation 假期 **jiàqí**
vacuum flask 保温瓶 **bǎowēnpíng**
vagina 阴道 **yīndào**
valid 有效 **yǒuxiào**
valley 山谷 **shāngǔ**
valuable 贵重 **guìzhòng**
valuables 贵重物品 **guìzhòng wùpǐn**
value 价值 **jiàzhí**
van 搬运车 **bānyùnchē**
vase 花瓶 **huāpíng**
vegetable 蔬菜 **shūcài**

vegetarian 吃素的 **chīsùde**
vein 血管／静脉 **xuèguǎn/jìngmài**
velvet 天鹅绒 **tiān'éróng**
vending machine 自动售货机 **zìdòng shòuhuòjī**
venereal disease 性病 **xìngbìng**
venomous 有毒的 **yǒudúde**
vertical 垂直的 **chuízhíde**
very 很 **hěn**
via 经由 **jīngyóu**
vicinity 附近 **fùjìn**
video camera 摄像机 **shèxiàngjī**
video cassette 摄像带 **shèxiàngdài**
video recorder 摄录机 **shèlùjī**
view 风景 **fēngjǐng**
village 村庄 **cūnzhuāng**
vinegar 醋 **cù**
visa 签证 **qiānzhèng**
visit 访问 **fǎngwèn**
visiting time 参观时间 **cānguān shíjiān**
vitamin tablets 维生素片 **wéishēngsùpiàn**
vitamins 维生素 **wéishēngsù**
volleyball 排球 **páiqiú**
vomit 呕吐 **ǒutù**
vulgar 粗俗的 **cūsúde**

W

wage 工资 **gōngzī**
waist 腰 **yāo**
wait 等 **děng**
waiter 男服务员 **nánfúwùyuán**
waiting room 候车室 **hòuchēshì**
waitress 女服务员 **nǚfúwùyuán**
wake 叫醒 **jiàoxǐng**
wake up 醒来 **xǐng lái**
walk (noun) 散步 **sànbù**

walk (verb) 走 **zǒu**

walking stick 拐杖 **guǎizhàng**

wall 墙 **qiáng**

wallet 钱包 **qiánbāo**

want 要 **yào**

war 战争 **zhànzhēng**

warm 温暖的 **wēnnuǎnde**

warn (verb) 警告 **jǐnggào**

warning 警告 **jǐnggào**

wash 洗 **xǐ**

washing 要洗的衣服 **yào xǐ de yīfu**

washing machine 洗衣机 **xǐyījī**

washing powder 洗衣粉 **xǐyīfěn**

washing room 洗手间 **xǐshǒujiān**

watch (look after) 看管 **kānguǎn**

watch (wristwatch) 表 **biǎo**

watch out 小心 **xiǎoxīn**

water 水 **shuǐ**

waterfall 瀑布 **pùbù**

watermelon 西瓜 **xīguā**

waterproof 不透水的 **bútòushuǐde**

way (direction) 方向 **fāngxiàng**

way (method) 方法 **fāngfǎ**

we 我们 **wǒmen**

weak 弱 **ruò**

wealthy 有钱／富有的 **yǒuqián/fùyǒude**

wear (clothing) 穿 **chuān**

weather 天气 **tiānqì**

weather forecast 天气预报 **tiānqì yùbào**

wedding 婚礼 **hūnlǐ**

Wednesday 星期三 **Xīngqīsān**

week 星期 **xīngqī**

weekday 周日 **zhōurì**

weekend 周末 **zhōumò**

weigh (verb) 称 **chèng**

weigh out 称出 **chèngchū**

weight 重量 **zhòngliàng**

welcome 欢迎 **huānyíng**

well (good) 好 **hǎo**

well (for water) 井 **jǐng**

west 西边 **xībiān**

West (Occident) 西方 **Xīfāng**

Western style 西式 **Xīshì**

Westernized 西化的 **Xīhuàde**

wet 湿的 **shīde**

what? 什么 **shénme**

wheelchair 轮椅 **lúnyǐ**

when? 什么时候 **shénme shíhou**

where? 哪里／哪儿 **nǎli/nǎr**

which? 哪个 **nǎ ge**

wide 宽 **kuān**

white 白色 **báisè**

white wine 白葡萄酒／白酒 **bái pútaojiǔ/báijiǔ**

who? 谁 **shéi/shuí**

whose 谁的 **shéide/shuíde**

whole 全部／整个 **quánbù/zhěngge**

why? 为什么 **wèishéme**

wide-angle lens 广角镜 **guǎngjiǎojìng**

widow 寡妇 **guǎfù**

widower 鳏夫 **guānfū**

wife 妻子 **qīzi**

wildlife 野生动物 **yěshēng dòngwù**

willing 愿意 **yuànyì**

win 赢 **yíng**

wind 风 **fēng**

window (in room) 窗户 **chuānghu**

windscreen, windshield 挡风玻璃 **dǎngfēng bōlí**

windshield wiper 雨刷 **yǔshuā**

wine 葡萄酒 **pútaojiǔ**

winter 冬天 **dōngtiān**

wire 金属线 **jīnshǔxiàn**

wish 希望 **xīwàng**

withdraw (bank) 提款 **tíkuǎn**

without 没有 **méiyǒu**

witness 证人 **zhèngrén**

woman 女人 **nǚrén**

wonderful 好极了 **hǎojíle**

wood 木头 **mùtou**

wool (knitting) 毛线 **máoxiàn**

wool (material) 羊毛 **yángmáo**

word 词 **cí**

work 工作 **gōngzuò**

working day 工作天 **gōngzuò tiān**

world 世界 **shìjiè**

worried 担心 **dānxīn**

worse 更坏的／更差的 **gènghuàide/gèng chàde**

worst 最坏的／最差的 **zuìhuài de/zuìchà de**

worthwhile 值得 **zhíde**

wound 伤口 **shāngkǒu**

wrap 包 **bāo**

wrapping (paper) 包装纸 **bāozhuāngzhǐ**

wrench, spanner 扳手 **bānshǒu**

wrist 手腕 **shǒuwàn**

wristwatch 表 **biǎo**

write 写 **xiě**

write down 写下来 **xiěxiàlái**

writer 作家 **zuòjiā**

writing pad 写字本 **xiězìběn**

wrong 错的 **cuòde**

X

x-ray X光片子 **X guāng piànzi**

Y

year 年 **nián**

yellow 黄色 **huángsè**

yes 对 **duì**

yes, please (acceptance) 好啊 **hǎo a**

yesterday 昨天 **zuótiān**

you 你 **nǐ**

you (plural) 你们 **nǐmen**

you're welcome 不谢 **búxiè**

young 年轻 **niánqīng**

youth hostel 青年招待所 **qīngnián zhāodàisuǒ**

Z

zero 零 **líng**

zip 拉链 **lāliàn**

zip (verb) 扣上拉链 **kòushàng lāliàn**

zoo 动物园 **dòngwùyuán**